PRAISE FOR *THE CULTURE*

"Innovation is one of the most elusive things to achieve in a company and, in a vast majority of cases, it is not the result of technology or research: it is a matter of developing the right culture. This book, with a great mix of analysis, theory and cases, is definitely a nice way to get our minds around it."
Enrique Dans, Professor of Innovation, IE University

"A must-have for start-ups, entrepreneurs, business leaders and change agents. Read linearly, use as a toolbox or dip in and out."
Marcus Watson, CEO, Investor at Ground Control

"Weaves together facts, stories, thoughtful reflections and up-to-date information that helps us rethink how we can add value by challenging and improving cultural norms."
Michael G Jacobides, Professor and Sir Donald Gordon Chair of Entrepreneurship and Innovation, London Business School

"There are moments in history when everything comes together and evolution takes a giant leap forward. *The Culture Advantage* will change the way you think about culture and provide you with a ton of insights and ingredients to build an exciting culture that is future-proof."
Wim Focquet, Head of People and Culture, Gala Games

"This is a book for doers looking for an advantage in today's messy, ever-changing, exciting world."
Steven MacGregor, author, *The Daily Reset* and Professor of Health and Wellbeing, Glasgow School of Art

"In this book, Daniel makes several important points on how to create a culture through which we can thrive and flourish at work, making our organizations hubs of innovation and creativity."
Marcello Russo, Associate Professor of Organization, University of Bologna, and Director of the Global MBA, Bologna Business School

"An excellent read and highly recommended for all entrepreneurs and C-suite management."
Nabil Hadi, Co-Founder, Digital Nomad Labs

"Culture is everything. It is the bedrock of how every great feat is achieved. This book shares real-life, inspiring stories and brings you the questions that will help you reflect and create action for a successful future."
Nick Humphries, Founder and CEO, Train Effective

"A must-read book for business leaders who want to better understand the speed of change or the need to speedily change, to lead a successful organization."
John Gazal, former Head of Strategic Programme Management, Strategy and CEO Office at Santander UK

"Corporate culture is one of the most important yet confusing topics in business. *The Culture Advantage* is filled with examples and real-world advice on what culture means and how to harness it for real business value."
Josh Bersin, Global Industry Analyst

The Culture Advantage

Empowering your people to drive innovation

Daniel Strode

KoganPage

First published in Great Britain and the United States in 2022 by Kogan Page Limited

2nd Floor, 45 Gee Street	8 W 38th Street, Suite 902	4737/23 Ansari Road
London EC1V 3RS	New York, NY 10018	Daryaganj
United Kingdom		New Delhi 110002
www.koganpage.com		India

Kogan Page books are printed on paper from sustainable forests.

ISBNs

Hardback   978 1 3986 0678 4
Paperback   978 1 3986 0676 0
Ebook   978 1 3986 0677 7

British Library Cataloguing-in-Publication Data

A CIP record for this book is available from the British Library.

Library of Congress Control Number
2022024395

Typeset by Integra Software Services, Pondicherry
Printed and bound by CPI Group (UK) Ltd, Croydon CR0 4YY

CONTENTS

LIST OF FIGURES

ACKNOWLEDGEMENTS

A book, of course, is the work of the author, but mostly it is the work of others behind the scenes. And I would like to thank, with the most sincere thanks possible, my family first and foremost for their support during this journey: in fact for giving me the push to share this knowledge and my passion for a topic I hold close to my heart. Without their support, and significant nudges, to enable me to complete this project it would have been a non-starter: so thank you for the ever-increasing levels of support to make an idea become a reality. I love you all. Also a big thank you to my father, who got me excited about the concept of business management, thanks to his own company which went from zero to millions, many years before I went down the rabbit hole of culture and innovation. All of my mentors, colleagues and students, past and present, you have played your part too – in shaping my thinking, and teaching me a huge amount about this topic, so thank you.

Thank you to Géraldine Collard and Matt James, my editors, and the whole team at Kogan Page. Géraldine in particular, you saw the value this book could bring and supported me in its development journey, taking it from the approvals process through to where we are today: a physical (or digital) copy for people to read. Helping a first-time author through a process of writing may be rewarding, but it is probably frustrating in equal measures, so thank you for bearing with me during the process.

I am indebted to those of you who have taken the time from your busy schedules to be interviewed for the book, and help my research. There are many of you, and I want you to know that your contributions have always proven extremely helpful and the quality of this book would be far worse without you kindly giving up your time. As readers will appreciate, you are on the cutting edge of the culture topic, and your work is the real inspiration behind this project: so, keep doing what you are doing – your cultures of innovation are the blueprints and they will inspire us all to use culture as our competitive advantage. It is also worth noting that as you receive a copy of this book, it will be the first time you see your words quoted: and that has been deliberate – we have all agreed that it is impor-tant the reader is presented with the facts and insight into your actions, rather than a well-crafted press release about your company and your efforts; so thank you for trusting in the process and sharing so openly.

And finally, to the readers: you are the reason I wrote the book. Please feel free to contact me at www.danielstrode.com or on LinkedIn (at danstrodepeopleculturespeaker) or email me (dan.strode.linkedin@gmail.com) with your observations and comments, and please consider leaving a review on Amazon: your honest feedback and reviews will help readers find the right book for their needs. My goal has been to share advice and tips, but this book could never be comprehensive given the nature of the topic – so I would love you to get in touch. Thank you for taking the time to read these words; it means you certainly have the passion to change your companies and make sure innovation is a driving force: the world needs more people of your ilk.

Introduction

I have long been fascinated by innovation and culture. For many years now I have thrown myself into understanding what makes companies and individuals tick, and in every instance, I have found that culture is at the forefront of successful, innovative companies. Each time I come across a magazine, internet article, or pick up the business press I scour the pages looking for companies of all shapes and sizes and then dive deep into the rabbit hole to learn more about them. I research them, try to speak with them, visit them, get to know members of the team and really find out what makes them who they are, what makes them tick.

I have found that companies that innovate successfully and in a sustained manner, tend to *share common attributes*: common cultural principles or traits. Culture is the number one factor in driving innovation in companies of all shapes and sizes, across all geographies and industries. Of course, there are other important factors at play like having the right resources and skills in place, the tools, the processes and the human capital. But these factors have far less importance, as we will see, in the innovation process than most may think – and certainly the most innovative companies don't share these tools and processes with any level of consistency when compared to these cultural principles.

In this regard, culture is the advantage, it is the driver of innovation.

This book

Over the course of the coming chapters, we are going to explore these cultural principles, which when combined, make for a potent secret ingredient in your search for innovation. These core principles which are distilled down in each chapter. They are characteristics which have consistently appeared across my research into cultures within innovative companies, and in discussions with my wonderful and inspirational cohorts of students at various universities around the world and numerous business leaders.

We are going to go on a journey that takes us through the headquarters of The LEGO Group, in Billund, Denmark. We will travel around the globe to Shenzen, China, to peek inside the headquarters of Ping An, and then onto many other locations of titans of industry and small-scale start-ups (and everything in between) in the United States and further afield. It is in these places, and these companies, where we find the ingredients that help companies innovate in the best way possible, increasing their chances of success in the Fourth Industrial Revolution. We will also see that there is no reason why a corporate giant cannot innovate at the same scale or pace as a nimble young start-up: it really is an opportunity and ingredient for all.

As ever, there is no clear recipe, and what works for one company won't necessarily work for another – so the important thing for you to focus on as you read this book, is taking what you learn and applying it to your company, making the learning your own, and experimenting as you go.

The eight principles for a culture of innovation

I have found *eight consistent principles* relating to culture which can really be used to drive innovation. These are the imperatives that innovative companies put into action. They are:

1 Rethink your business model.

2 Create creativity with constraints.

3 Have a growth mindset.

4 Use the wisdom of crowds.

5 Embrace technology.

6 Hire well.

7 Put your people first.

8 Leaders, participate in culture.

The structure

Each chapter has a short introduction, and then is comprised of various mini case studies, short stories if you will. The idea of filling a book with these short stories is so that you, as the reader, will be able to learn from real-life examples in a deeply practical and accessible manner. The stories avoid major complexities, but provide enough knowledge and practical advice to set you well on your way.

Throughout the book there are also a number of interviews and contributions from people who are experts in their fields, and have used these eight imperatives to their advantage.

At the end of each chapter, you will find a series of questions for reflection. These are important, and I encourage you to write in the book or on a piece of paper: scribble your thoughts and reflections – this will help with the learning process. A number of the questions will lead you to action, based upon your answers – and that will be a good thing.

Before we look at each of the eight principles or traits, we start with a brief summary of innovation and culture. And then after the eight principles have been discussed we close with a recap and reminder.

Hard things take effort

You will have to be consistent in your application of culture, as we will see in the following chapters, as *this isn't a quick fix*. In the same way that brushing your teeth is good for you, so is building a solid company culture. And you need to take the same approach: brushing your teeth twice a day for two minutes, with a level of absolute consistency, will leave you with sparkling white teeth. Whereas brushing your teeth for an hour once a week simply won't cut it. Culture is the same – it takes time and sustained effort.

As with most things, the hard things are the most rewarding, and a challenge to implement, or shift. A company culture will be one of your hardest, but most rewarding, challenges.

I wish you the very best of luck in these exciting times. I hope you will implement the culture advantage in your companies and use culture as your competitive and sustainable advantage over your competitors. I know a great culture will empower your people to drive innovation and lead to great success in your chosen fields. So, let us begin…

01

The culture advantage

Culture eats strategy for breakfast.

PETER DRUCKER, AMERICAN MANAGEMENT GURU

The pace of change

The pace of change has never been so fast. Yet, it will never be as slow in the future as it is today.

With the wonderful medical advances that have been happening in recent years, not least vaccines, we see that the average human lifespan in developed countries is north of 80 years, with men born today being expected to live until 79 years of age, and women to 82 years on average. We have seen a global and sustained uptick from an average lifespan at birth of 69.9 years in 2008 to 72.75 years in 2019 (O'Neill, 2021b). There is nothing to suggest that this trend is going to reverse any time soon. Some wonderful advances in human longevity are on the cusp, with genomic sequencing, stem cell therapy, CRISPR, and human microbiome technologies coming to the market on a near daily basis: these are technologies and breakthroughs that will revolutionize our lives, and our health.

Healthcare, which has until recently solely been focused on 'sick care', i.e. taking care of people when they are unwell, is now focusing on 'wellness care', where smart technology on your wristwatch (or other connected Internet of Things device) which is keeping an eye on your heart rate, blood pressure, breathing, weight and activity levels, suggests small adjustments to keep you in peak condition. From being reactive when we fall ill, we are now in a mode of maintenance, always looking after ourselves, with the ultimate goal of reducing those reactive moments when things go wrong.

Whilst the outlook for humans is wonderful, and will continue to be, the reverse of the human lifespan growth is being seen in corporate lifespans, which are dropping at an alarming rate. I am not talking about start-ups and new businesses, which we all know have a shockingly high failure rate. I am talking about top companies – giants of industry. These companies in 1960 outlived humans on average by ten years (the human lifespan being around the 50-year mark, whilst these titans of industry could live to around 60 years (Credit Suisse, 2017)). This phenomenon has completely been flipped on its head. As of today, the most successful companies, according to market capitalization and the fact they are listed on major stock indexes such as the S&P 500, live to around 21 years old (Clark, 2021).

Given that Amazon was founded in 1994, Google in 1996, Netflix in 1997 and Twitter in 2006, statistically speaking some of these must soon be coming to the ends of their lives, unless they can find the magic cure and continue to re-invent themselves. Which, I will argue, they have been able to do so far – and this book takes inspiration from them, amongst others.

The Fourth Industrial Revolution

As the world changes, the pressure on companies to succeed ramps up a notch. No one wants to become extinct. The reality is, however, that in a hyper-connected world, few succeed as competition is fierce and there is no hiding place. We have entered the Fourth Industrial Revolution: a golden time for consumers and a very stressing time for companies.

In the First Industrial Revolution we saw water and steam power being used in order to boost production. The Second Industrial Revolution saw humans use electric power to mass-produce things, and the Third Industrial Revolution started to automate that production by using advanced electronics and computer systems.

We are now firmly living in the Fourth Industrial Revolution, and it is hyper-charged. Technologies such as artificial intelligence (AI), augmented and virtual reality (AR and VR), data science, biological advances and biotech, nanotech robotics, 5G and blockchains would individually herald a new revolution of their own. However, they are taking place in parallel to one another, and even more exciting is that they are converging to create exponential growth. Of course, you will know given the December 2019 outbreak of Covid-19 what exponential means: it's the same effect as the effect of compounding in finance, or the effect of a pyramid scheme (or Ponzi scheme) where one investor invites two more, and those two invite four more, with growth happening at a frightening rate. Growth, and change, has never been so fast, nor will it remain as slow ever again.

The need to innovate

So, companies find themselves with the need to innovate. Because, if they do not, they will likely fall foul of the Fourth Industrial Revolution. Irrespective of what industry you are in, change is happening around you.

If you are in banking, you will have noticed an increasing amount of time being spent online by your customers, which leads you to needing powerful mobile banking platforms. You will have also seen customer expectations shifting dramatically, and no longer are you being compared to your peers but you are being compared to Amazon. Customers are wondering why it takes seven working days for a new debit card to be sent to them in the post, when their groceries can be delivered within just two hours by Amazon. New technologies available in the Fourth Industrial Revolution have converged and new entrants are eating your value chain and attacking your business model. Many of them are small start-ups, but big technology companies like Apple and Facebook are joining the party too: they attack your payments business, the most profitable part of your industry for a long time, and do it with such low overheads they are bound to win unless you can change and adapt. Unless you can innovate.

If you happen to be in the food industry, you are also facing imposed changes to your business. New entrants in the form of local producers are taking market share. New business models are showing up based on a demand for sugar-free products, sustainable food sources and affordability. Again, customer expectations have changed and people are demanding healthy, personalized and fast meal choices. The world is shifting under your feet, and again, unless you can innovate you may find yourself in a tricky situation sooner than you think.

The good news is that the human race is pretty good, as a whole, at innovating, adapting and evolving. Charles Darwin's theory of evolution states that evolution happens by natural selection. Thus, over time, those individuals most suited to their environment survive, and, given even longer periods of time, the species as a whole gradually evolves.

On a company level, people make the company, and thus companies innovate, adapt and evolve too – as long as they act and behave in the right way. If not, they face extinction.

Types of innovation

Innovation is the implementation and execution of ideas that enables new goods or services to come to market, or existing goods or services to improve or be enhanced. What you innovate can take place on many fronts:

- It may be that your company innovates upon its *business model*: changing the way you operate. For example, Netflix moving from DVD rentals to an online streaming service.
- You may also be undertaking *market innovation*: you could introduce a new idea which creates a whole new market, like the iPhone did when it created the world of smartphones. Or, you could enter a new market that your company hasn't traditionally been a part of. Think Amazon, a humble bookstore, which is now a global marketplace, media company, cloud computing provider, and much more.
- Perhaps *product innovation* is your thing: you are busy developing and offering new products and solutions to your customers, things they have never experienced before. Consider how your car may have already turned from petrol to diesel to electric, or shortly will.
- And, finally, you may be looking at *service innovation*: enhancing the offering to your customers, as is the case in banking, with the digital race for the best mobile experience.

How to innovate

How to innovate is the multi-billion-dollar question. There is often no right or wrong way, but rather a set of ingredients that can help, and a secret ingredient that acts as the catalyst and magic to the baking.

As always, there is no clear answer – what works for one company may not work for another. But there are regular patterns repeated across successful companies. They are:

- a *clear strategy*
- a *malleable business* structure

- a secret ingredient and your competitive advantage: a powerful *culture of innovation*

The first pillar of building innovation is the need to have a very clear strategy and set of frameworks and principles for innovation in your company. Your strategy should set out what type of innovation you want to do (business model innovation, market innovation, product innovation or service innovation), and then how you do it – no need to be running around like a headless chicken, expecting to innovate and find the next big business idea through sheer luck and chance. Unless you are a start-up, you will often have to choose how you innovate alongside running your existing business lines, and decisions will need to be made about resource allocation and the types of innovation you pursue. They could be:

- *routine* and day-to-day innovations, i.e. incremental product improvements
- or *disruptive innovations* where you flip a business model on its head, like Uber did to ride sharing
- or, you might pursue *radical innovation*, which requires you to change competencies within your organization (think cars moving from petrol/diesel to electric)
- and finally, you may pursue a kind of *structural innovation*, where a changing business model is combined with changing competencies as in the case of Kodak: a digitalization of the product, which implied a competency change from film to digital, changed both the product and the model. Kodak no longer received income from films, processing and services but rather from digital storage.

The second pillar is your business structure or organizational structure, and a very relevant input.

- Many companies set up *separate entities* for their innovation efforts, free of corporate interference and bureaucracy.
- Many choose to *co-create solutions with their customers*, like MasterCard Labs who build prototypes and solutions with their customers, building lasting relationships.
- Others turn to what could be called a *portfolio approach*, like Alphabet Inc. takes with its innovation: Google remains the core business, and separate ventures like DeepMind (their AI business) and X (their research facility) operate as part of a wider portfolio of investments or bets.

- Whilst others run *incubators*, which nurture ideas such as the highly successful Bayer Grant4Apps programme, which has become a global phenomenon for the pharmaceutical giant.

The point being, there are too many structures and models to list; the structure you put in place could be one of many choices, and you have chances to succeed as long as you take one approach and commit to it.

We then get to the third, and most, important pillar. The secret ingredient – the one that gives you your competitive advantage.

The secret ingredient

The secret ingredient to innovation is culture. You can have wonderful ingredients like the fanciest campuses in the world, you can have the most money to throw at research and development, and you can hire mavericks from all over the world with the best individual talent: but, if you can't mix it all together, you will not be able to bake the cake.

Culture, from the Latin word *Cultus*, which translated means 'care', is, as you can see, a very people-focused word. A word which puts people at the centre, and in a very positive, caring way (Berger, 2000).

To academics, there are various definitions for culture, and specifically company or corporate culture. However, to me, *the most simple and clear definition I can give is that culture is 'the way we do things around here, when no one is looking'.* The last part of that sentence is very important; culture has to be in your DNA and you can't force it. You have to create an environment where it can grow and reinforce itself, and it's notoriously difficult to change: but it can be done. It doesn't work, however, when you are trying to game the system and force culture on to the organization; it has to be organic and well-intentioned.

Let me give perhaps the best example. A popular TV series called *The Good Place* is about a set of people who find themselves, after death, in 'the good place' where everything is meant to be like a paradise and they live their life after death happily ever after. However, as events transpire, it becomes clear that they are being tricked and actually they're living in 'the bad place' where the colleagues are just annoying enough to keep them on the edge of unhappiness. They have only one way to escape and gain safe passage to the real good place, and that is by becoming better people, changing their behaviours – through the act of helping, caring, supporting one another. However, if they become better people for the sake of getting into the good place they will never achieve the goal, as their motivation is driven by their own intrinsic will to win for themselves. The only way to achieve the goal is to become better people because that is the right thing to do. And with culture, it's much the same. We have to do things in a specific way, when no one is looking, because it's the right thing to do. You can't fake it, it simply won't work.

Many companies try to build a great culture, perhaps even a culture of innovation, by placing bean bags in the hallways, having a hundred different flavours of drinks in the free vending machine, hiring Michelin-starred chefs to cook lunch for employees and a whole set of other, nice-to-have perks (which of course have their place). They don't, however, make up an honest and genuine culture. Companies do this for a number of reasons. Perhaps an expensive external consultant has told them they need to improve morale and pool tables will help, but most of the time they fall into this trap because culture-building is difficult. Let us be very clear with one another – it is hard. There are no shortcuts or overnight successes. It will require consistent work and effort, and your reward may only become apparent some years later.

As well as this 'social culture' of behaviours, a company of course needs to have a strong and well-executed strategy (the right products, technology, market, etc) to thrive. This strategy, coupled with the 'technical culture' of aligned reward systems, processes, structures and definitions of company missions and goals by the executive team, combined with the social/behavioural elements, will be the main indicator of your success.

Unfortunately for those wanting a quick fix, this won't be your answer: you can't take a PowerPoint presentation to your executive team on a Thursday and have the outcome by Friday, as you might with the change in pricing of one of your products. However, if you do it right, it will be the most sustainable answer and most important competitive advantage you can build into the DNA of your company.

I say that culture is the sustainable advantage because – in my view – a company is somewhat like a computer system. It is formed of two main parts: firstly the hardware and secondly the software. The hardware is the technical knowledge, machines, buildings and various other parts of a business – and anyone can copy or reverse engineer this part, given enough time and resources. The software, however, is the advantage because it is unique to you, unique to your company and it is exactly this culture that you have in your DNA that acts as the catalyst and magic to your success.

There are many facets to culture

If we turn now to academia, there are hundreds of definitions for culture. Far too many to count, indeed; even way back in 1952 when anthropologists from the United States, Krober, Kluckhohn and Untereiner, counted them, they found 164 different definitions (Kroeber et al, 1952). I don't propose to do a re-count, but have no doubts this has increased since the 1950s, especially as culture has become a topic very much in vogue, in more recent years.

However, in my opinion, there is one predominant model which explains, or frames academically, what culture is: the cultural web model by Gerry Johnson. This is the pre-eminent model, in my view, to explain what comprises the field of culture, what makes a culture. It has stood the test of time, with academics relying on the insight for the past 30 or so years, with subsequent research aligning to the findings it presented. I thoroughly enjoy Johnson's model, as it is truly accessible and sets out a very straightforward construct, which I hope you the reader will quickly grasp. With a clear frame around what culture is comprised of, we will be able to better understand the unique DNA of a company.

Gerry Johnson created the cultural web model to help individuals and companies understand what culture is. Gerry kindly produced the following explanation of the web, specifically for you, the reader of this book, to accompany Figure 1.1 and share in detail the components of the cultural web. It appears in *Exploring Corporate Strategy* (Johnson et al, 2017) and is reproduced with the permission of Gerry Johnson.

THE CULTURAL WEB: SUMMARY OF COMPONENTS

Organizational culture is the taken-for-granted assumptions and behaviours of an organization's members. This culture helps make sense of people's organizational context and therefore contributes to how they respond to issues they face. It therefore typically influences the strategy of an organization and can be very resistant to change. The cultural web is a way of understanding an organization's culture.

Taken-for-granted assumptions are the core of an organization's culture. In the cultural web this is referred to as the *paradigm – the set of assumptions held in common and taken for granted in an organization.* These core assumptions guide how people view and respond to different circumstances they face. They are, quite likely, very basic and apparently straightforward. For example, quite commonly in technology and engineering firms there is the propensity of people to focus on the technical excellence of products rather than customer-perceived needs. Medical practitioners tend to take for granted the primary importance of curing illnesses. Professors in universities take for granted the importance of research. The police take for granted the importance of social order. None of these are surprising and should not be. The point is that because they are taken for granted and likely to be very embedded, changing them, if change is required, is extremely difficult.

It is quite likely that, even if a rational view is to build a strategy around the engineering business' customer needs or the need for prevention (as distinct from curing) of illnesses, people in those organizations may still interpret issues and behave in line with its paradigm. So understanding what the paradigm is and how it informs debate on strategy matters. The problem is that, since it is unlikely to be talked about, or even be something that people are conscious of, trying to identify it is difficult, especially if you are part of that organization. Outside observers may find it easier to identify simply by listening to what people say and emphasize. One way of 'insiders' getting to see the assumptions they take for granted is to focus initially on other aspects of the cultural web. These, too, may well be taken for granted but they are more visible manifestations of culture:

- *Routines* are 'the way we do things around here' on a day-to-day basis. At their best, routines lubricate the working of an organization. However, they can also represent a taken-for-grantedness about how things should happen which, again, can guide how people deal with situations and be difficult to change. For example, managers trying to achieve greater customer focus in engineering firms often report that customer-facing sales engineers routinely tend to tell customers what they need rather than listening to their needs.

- Organizational *rituals* are when people step out of their routines. This may, however, be in order to emphasize, highlight or reinforce what is important in the culture. Examples include training programmes, interview panels, promotion and assessment procedures, sales conferences and so on. An extreme example, of course, is the ritualistic training of army recruits to prepare them for the discipline required in conflict. However, rituals can also be informal activities such as drinks in the pub after work or gossiping around water-coolers.

- The *stories* told by members of an organization to each other, to outsiders or to new recruits can act to embed the present in its organizational history, let people know what is conventionally important in an organization, and also flag up important events and personalities. They typically have to do with successes, disasters, heroes, villains and mavericks (who deviate from the norm).

- *Symbols* are objects, events, acts or people that convey, maintain or create meaning over and above their functional purpose. For example, offices and office layout, cars and job titles have a functional purpose, but are also typically signals about status and hierarchy. Particular people may come to represent especially important aspects of an organization or historic turning points. The language used in an organization can also be particularly revealing, especially with regard to customers or clients: defining executive education clients as 'course participants' rather than 'students' makes a significant difference to how teaching staff interact with them. Although symbols are shown separately in the cultural web, it should be remembered that many elements of the web are symbolic. So, routines, control and reward systems and structures are not only functional but also symbolic.

- *Power* is the ability of individuals or groups to persuade, induce or coerce others into following certain courses of action. So *power structures* are distributions of power to groups of people in an organization. The most powerful individuals or groups are likely to be closely associated with the paradigm and long-established ways of doing things.

- *Organizational structures* are the roles, responsibilities and reporting relationships in organizations. These are likely to reflect power structures and how they manifest themselves. Formal hierarchical, mechanistic structures may emphasize that strategy is the province of top managers. Structures with less emphasis on formal reporting relationships might indicate more participative strategy making. Highly decentralized structures may signify that collaboration is less important than competition and so on.

- *Control systems* are the formal but also informal ways of monitoring and supporting people within and around an organization and tend to emphasize what is seen to be important in the organization. They include measurements and reward systems. For example, public-service organizations have often been accused of being concerned more with stewardship of funds than with quality of service. This is reflected in their control systems, which are often more about accounting for spending rather than with quality of service.

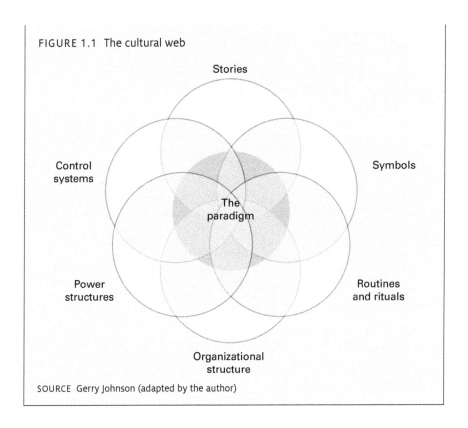

FIGURE 1.1 The cultural web

SOURCE Gerry Johnson (adapted by the author)

Now we know the elements, we can explore how to change them.

Changing culture is hard

Changing culture is not easy; it takes time and deliberate effort. As we see with the cultural web model, there are core elements of a culture. Using this insight, and other academic references, I propose that when it comes to changing cultures, and specifically behaviours, there are five key elements to focus on in order to have underlying change within a company, which you can see in Figure 1.2.

The five aspects to change the culture within a company are:

1 *Leadership:* Leaders have to be role models, and live the culture each day, without fail.

2 *Communications:* The company must explain clearly the culture and the reasons for it.

3 *Competencies:* Training needs to take place in order to support people to manage the change and ensure that they are equipped with the skills needed to make it a success.

4 *Measurement and reward:* Once people have the tools, measurement must be put in place to ensure progress and rewards can be allocated in line with the culture.

5 *Operations:* Finally, as a company changes, the changing culture must be reflected in changes within the business, in terms of new rituals, symbols and processes being put in place.

FIGURE 1.2 How to change culture: The culture change model

SOURCE Author

These themes are woven into the coming chapters, and you will be able to see examples of companies who do well in each of these aspects.

Though it is difficult, the effort will be worth it in the end. Culture is important to ensuring your long-term, sustainable success in innovation moving forwards.

It is important

If you still don't believe culture is important, why not take the advice of Warren Buffett, the legendary investor and Chairman of Berkshire Hathaway, who said in a letter to Berkshire Hathaway managers in 2006 'culture, more than rule books, determines how an organization behaves' and this quote is so true (*Financial Times*, 2006).

Also take notice of what your investors want to hear about. Gartner research shows that during earnings calls with large corporate companies since 2010 the most discussed topic is company culture, with mentions of culture increasing by 7 per cent annually (Gartner, 2019). With companies talking about culture externally and investors being more interested than ever before in the organizations' culture, it is incumbent upon leaders to safeguard their firm's reputation, its success and its culture.

If your investors are not ringing bells, why not consider your regulators. Regulators are also looking at corporate cultures. Think about the cases when culture goes wrong, and the impacts it can have.

In recent memory, and with regulatory interest, we only have to consider the case of Enron in December 2001: the biggest accounting scandal in history with the company, a provider of natural gas and energy, being the poster child of the stock market for many years until filing for bankruptcy when the accounting scandal, driven by an aggressive culture of misrepresentation and mis-selling amongst other suspect practices, became public. With over sixty billion dollars of assets, it was the largest bankruptcy case at the time (Benston, 2003). The damaging culture at Enron also took down the accountants Arthur Andersen.

Still, companies haven't paid as much attention to their cultures as they should have. Volkswagen, the German car manufacturer, sold diesel cars around the world (about eleven million of them in total) which had 'defeat devices' fitted to their exhausts in order to cheat the results of emissions tests. This irregularity came to light and in 2015 Volkswagen admitted the charges. With their culture lacking psychological safety, employees cheated the system rather than telling their bosses the car designs were not emission-friendly enough (Ruddick, 2015). Since then, Volkswagen has made relentless efforts to improve the overall culture within the organization, and specifically the compliance culture, with a whistleblower hotline and the introduction of compliance officers in each division now in place across the world, amongst other changes.

And finally, in September 2020, the United States House Committee on Transportation and Infrastructure, which we will discuss at length later in the book, cited the catastrophic Boeing 737MAX crashes, which rocked the world of aviation, as being down to a complex series of actions and events – whilst mentioning the word 'culture' no less than sixty times in their report

(United States House Committee on Transportation and Infrastructure, 2020). The impacts of cultural failings in this case were disastrous.

These, sadly, are just a few. Fortunately though, there are many wonderful success stories about companies who innovate in the right way and thrive in the long term, delighting their bands of loyal customers along the way.

Make the cake rise

We have now established that change is happening around us, at breakneck speeds. I've posited that our only chance of survival is to innovate, adapt and evolve – as has always been the case.

We also now know that there are plenty of ways to do this, but with no clear recipe for guaranteed success.

However, all of the ways to innovate have one secret ingredient that makes the cake rise: culture.

QUESTIONS FOR REFLECTION

- What does it feel like currently to work in your company? What is the culture?
- What would you like it to feel like to work in your company, in the future?
- What actions do you need to take in order to make it feel like you want it to? What are the barriers, hurdles, and challenges you need to overcome?

In the next chapter we are going to take a look at business models, and learn about one of the key mental attitudes we can have to encourage innovation to thrive. We are going to look at how to create a culture where challenging the status quo is normal, and see how being receptive to change in our business models and operations is vital so we don't fall into common traps, such as outcome bias where we think we are doing fantastically well and our success will continue. Because, when you have that attitude, you can be sure a surprise is just around the corner, and it's unlikely to be a nice one.

02

Rethink your business model

If everything seems under control, you're not going fast enough.
MARIO ANDRETTI, FORMULA ONE, INDYCAR, WORLD
SPORTSCAR CHAMPIONSHIP AND NASCAR RACE WINNER

So, as we start with the first of the principles we begin the core of this journey. We are going to explore the mindset of a company, and what individuals within it need, in order to drive innovation. In this chapter we are going to explore one of the most important mindset shifts you can make in order to build a culture where innovation thrives. But, one that is perhaps the most difficult to successfully implement because of its counterintuitive nature.

We are going to look at why it is important that you have a culture of challenging the status quo and, specifically, rethinking your business model and its underlying assumptions. We will look at some of the most famous case studies in business management history, of companies who have failed to adjust with the times, and others who have adjusted well and pivoted into new business models and ways of operating.

No one stays in their lane

As we saw in the previous chapter, the world is changing fast in this Fourth Industrial Revolution. With technologies converging, leading to exponential changes, *businesses need to be questioning their beliefs and ways of acting.*

Just like driving through the streets of Madrid during rush hour, *no one stays in their lane* any longer, and they especially don't indicate when they do change lanes. It is the same with people – no one stays in their lane any longer either. People are rethinking their careers. There used to be a time, not so long ago, where employees would take a job and sit back for their entire careers in the same company, slowly (or not) working their way up the corporate ladder before retiring with gold-plated pensions. This is no longer the case, not least due to the changing composition of the workforce and different expectations that new generations have: they want multiple careers in different companies, more rapid career growth and the ability to experience new things. And, finally, the half-life of skills that are required by employers is being completely eroded, which means there is simply no choice but to reinvent yourself multiple times over in your career.

The same goes for companies. Most companies no longer stay in their lane. Many are *rethinking their business models constantly*. Amazon started as an online book store in July 1994, and as of 2021 Amazon not only sells books but own-brand products, hosts third-party vendors, provides web services and cloud-based computing solutions, co-brands credit cards with major financial institutions, operates physical shop locations, and offers subscription services on demand which span from video (much of which is content created by in-house studios), through to music and reading to name but just a few. It isn't just Amazon, of course, it's everybody and anybody out there – Apple are well in on the act, moving into digital payments and healthcare, with watches that you can use to pay for your coffee using Apple Pay and, at the same time as spending your money, track your heart rate to make sure nothing is amiss either with your dwindling bank balance or the caffeine in your coffee!

When individuals and companies both decide not to stay in their lane and instead opt to rethink their own skills and their business models, really curious (and exciting) things happen. Take Gary Vaynerchuk, or Gary Vee as he is commonly known. As of 2021 he is a 46-year-old entrepreneur. In 1998, fresh out of school, Gary Vee took charge of his family's business, a liquor shop. The business was doing great; it was the hard work of his family that had started the business and turned it into an annual $3 million turnover business. Step by step, Gary Vee undertook a massive transformation of the business. His first step was renaming it 'Wine Library' rather than its rather lacklustre early name 'Shopper's Discount Liquors'. He jumped onto the social media bandwagon that was in its infancy and built Wine Library TV, where he would talk about wines that matched with various types of food, and all sorts of topics related to wine. It became a daily show and it propelled the business from its $3 million turnover to a $60 million turnover by the time he left and handed over the reins in 2011 (Vaynerchuk, 2017b). Gary Vee had clearly spent his time innovating and transforming the business model, to take advantage of social media.

What happened next was most interesting. He founded, in 2009, VaynerMedia, which is now a highly successful advertising agency with flagship adverts shown at half-time during the Super Bowl, and spawning various viral successes online for those who work with the company. Step by step, this company has grown and gone from strength to strength, and it now falls under the VaynerX holding company which has spun off various businesses from news outlets like ONE37pm, to VaynerTalent, which is a talent agency for sports stars, through to the Sasha Group, which provides education and consulting services to help brands grow.

Why is this interesting? Well, because every time Gary Vee is interviewed about his rise through the ranks of business, he shares the same story. Naysayers always told him that he wouldn't be successful with his new and latest venture, and they would tell him to 'stay in your lane, wine boy' – he wasn't expected or allowed to venture outside of his lane, his comfort zone and certainly wasn't given permission to change his business interests and models by others.

In 2021, Gary Vee has made his boldest and probably to-be-most-successful breakaway from his lane so far. He has rethought his business model once again and moved into the world of NFTs. NFTs stands for 'non-fungible tokens', which are units of data that are stored on digital ledgers called the blockchain. The tokens are digital assets that live online, and are linked to digital art, collectibles, gaming and many more things. These assets can be sold and traded online using cryptocurrency.

You will recall that the blockchain was one of the exponential technologies mentioned in the previous chapter, and here we have a great example of an individual, and their company, moving lane and rethinking their business model, from being a wine merchant in a physical shop in New Jersey to becoming wildly successful in a completely different lane: creating intellectual property online with things that 'only' exist on the blockchain, not even physically. His first NFT project, named VeeFriends, is a series of collectable tokens (with very cool characters) hand-drawn by Gary Vee himself which also act as redeemable vouchers for events such as conferences, or FaceTime sessions with Gary Vee and his team, or the chance to hang out at a lunch event with him (VeeFriends, 2021). Over time, the mission is to build the intellectual property around the VeeFriends and thus use the characters in films, magazines or merchandizing.

NFTs are no flash in the pan. In 2021 the digital artist Beetle sold one piece, yes, just one piece, of digital art for $69 million (Christie's, 2021). And the market isn't showing signs of a slowdown just yet. So, with that in mind, Gary Vee also launched VayerNFT to help corporate giants take advantage of the emerging technology offered by the blockchain and create long-term value for their brands and communities. His VaynerX holding company, and subsidiaries within it, are in this constant state of flux and transformation, always adapting to trends in the markets, or setting new trends ahead of time.

Gary Vee's rise through multiple careers, multiple interests and multiple successes clearly is a result of the wine boy *not* staying in his lane, and being brave and bold enough to rethink on a continual basis his business models. Of course, Gary Vee doesn't do this alone, and has built this curiosity and culture of change into his companies, with his people continually tasked to search for new opportunities and ways to pivot the business or enter a new lane. Within VaynerX, they ask *'Why not?' instead of 'Why?'* and find that this simple question enables them to think outside of the box, and helps to pivot and transform their businesses (Vaynerchuk, 2020).

One great anecdote of how Gary Vee has infused this culture of challenging the status quo can be seen when people leave VaynerX companies. The first thing managers do is say 'thank you' and 'congratulations' to those who are leaving, as they are going on to try new things in their life, and it's true that the culture encourages people to 'rock the boat' (both in your individual career, and within the company). With a culture of 'risk taking' to 'avoid being stagnant', people have permission to push the boundaries, and change their lane (Vaynerchuk, 2017a).

The curious case of Blockbuster and Netflix

So, given we have just seen the example of VaynerX and Gary Vee changing their lanes, constantly and effectively, why isn't this happening all of the time and why is this not actually that easy to do?

As a child I remember visiting the local Blockbuster store with my mother on a very regular basis. I remember the distinctive blue and yellow membership card, the Blockbuster logo, and the walls jam-packed with video tapes of the latest releases, most of which I wasn't allowed to watch as they were above my age recommendation.

This weekly pilgrimage to Blockbuster, which I am sure many of you are familiar with if you lived through the 1990s, was fun. You would browse the shelves, choose your movie, take the empty video box to the counter and the attendant would find the video tape in the storeroom and place it into the box for you to take home for the number of days you had asked to rent it for. If you were lucky, you might also take home some popcorn for your movie and any number of little extras that Blockbuster enticed you with. Of course, if you went over the number of days you were meant to keep the video there were hefty charges to pay, which made sense in terms of a business decision, as Blockbuster only had a window of a few weeks to keep churning the video tapes of the latest films to as many customers as possible before the next batch of Hollywood releases came out and customers lost interest in the older movies.

This was one of the most wonderful companies in the world, one that was dominating the industry, nearly unchallenged. Each local competitor was systematically wiped off of the map by Blockbuster; their economies of scale and hard bargaining positions led to independent video stores closing in their droves, or being bought up by Blockbuster. It is said that at one point 90 per cent of all Americans were within a ten-minute drive of a Blockbuster video store (Ash, 2020). However, that was about to change in the early 2000s.

Blockbuster, which was sold to Viacom in 1994 for $8.4 billion (Black, 1994) was about to head in an altogether different direction. This was thanks to a small company called Netflix, who were undertaking rapid business model innovation, which many say Blockbuster should have been doing themselves – but their culture didn't allow it.

It was tough for Blockbuster; they were a multi-billion-dollar company doing great. They were opening in more and more locations, their international expansion was going well and they were the dominant force. Culturally they had, however, fallen short, with senior management not aware of what was about to happen. Especially because of their success, they thought they would continue being successful and having the Midas touch. As late as 2008, the CEO of Blockbuster at the time, Jim Keyes, told journalists that 'Neither RedBox nor Netflix are even on the radar screen in terms of competition' (Munarriz, 2008). The company continued to see things that way until their demise in 2010 when they filed for bankruptcy.

Netflix, in contrast, was an up-and-coming start-up which was launched by Reed Hastings in 1997. DVDs were slowly replacing video tapes and more family homes were installing DVD players and connecting them to their televisions. DVDs had been invented in 1995 and Reed had spotted an opportunity. Netflix's first act began with customers in 1998 and they offered them DVDs by mail order. The films were older, lesser-known films, which were inexpensive for Netflix to acquire because demand was lower than it was for the big blockbuster (pardon the pun) films of the day. Netflix went on a buying spree and bought many films before launching a website which helped customers choose which film to watch – and this was important as many customers hadn't heard of the obscure and non-blockbuster films they were stocking. This website had an algorithm running behind it which directed customers to films they would like, and the more information you gave the website, and greater viewing history you had, the better the algorithm could do and over time the recommendations would get stronger and stronger. Netflix was matching the tastes and needs of customers to the stock it was holding.

Now, customers could rent DVDs online, direct from the website, instead of travelling to their nearest Blockbuster store and physically retrieving a video tape (or DVD, which Blockbuster too started to stock). Convenience was key in this, and customers loved the fact they could keep the films for as long as they wanted without any additional charge by way of late fee, and when they were done, return them using the post. The United States Postal Service became Netflix's best friend, as they were creating huge value by way of convenience for customers. I still remember 'borrowing' my parents, credit card to sign up to Netflix and order DVDs online: the distinctive white jiffy bag arriving in the morning's post with just a DVD inside (no case) and a pre-paid reply envelope was always exciting to open, despite knowing what movie was inside.

Netflix shifted from pay-per-rental to a model of monthly subscription, which later became the bedrock of its growth and financial performance. By the time Netflix shifted its model once again in 2007, continually having a culture of rethinking its business model and executing on it, to offer video on demand technology to customers, i.e. streaming of films online using the internet, Blockbuster had all but faded away from the corporate landscape.

As Netflix turned its attention away from the United States Postal Service and set its sights on the broadband streaming cables that run under the ground and our oceans, Hastings and the Netflix team were warned by investors and external critics not to change the business model as moving from the DVD rental by post model to an online streaming model would cannibalize their profits and lead Netflix to lose out on existing customer revenue. Which, in the short term, was correct – they did lose out on revenues and there was cannibalization of their DVD rental by post business.

However, in the longer term, without the need to move physical disks across the country (and all the distribution and logistics needed), and store them in an expensive inventory (big warehouses and security), Netflix was set for hyper-growth. No longer with the burden of inventory management and distribution around its neck, which actually was extremely complex and led to various cash crunches during the growth stage of the company, Netflix was free to grow its offering. And that, it did.

Netflix bought the rights to as much content as it could, old and new. The bigger the library, the better. Customers had instant access to on-demand video content and it was unlimited, in line with its monthly subscription model – with movies played on the customers' computer or television screen as they wished. This led to more customer growth and more demand, and the second act of the Netflix story was closing with more success thanks to its culture of innovation and its willingness to rethink its business model, cannibalize its own business lines, and embrace technology as a partner. They didn't *fall into the trap of believing that the success they had created so far would take them into the future successfully* and they continued to push and challenge common business assumptions.

The third act, which is playing out now, saw Amazon Prime Video, Apple TV, Disney+, HBO Max, Vimeo and a whole host of other content streaming firms emerge as online platforms. With an experience driven by the famous algorithm to help you choose what to watch, the battle has moved from the best inventory and logistics, to the most convenient customer service and advice on what movies to watch, to the battle for original content.

The firms in this space are now battling for customers and adding value through original content – that is, content created by or for the companies in question. When Amazon was competing with Apple for the same movies as Netflix there was a crunch on prices and everything rose, with customers being the ones worse off. Much like football rights in the UK when Amazon Prime went to battle with Sky TV, the winners were the creators of the content, the football clubs. When football in the United Kingdom was first aired on commercial television channels, the cost was £232 million in 1992 and this has now risen, in a pandemic environment, to £9.1 billion, which is a rise of nearly 4,000 per cent (Davis, 2021).

So, with content prices rising, Netflix (and others) have switched their business models once more to create in their own production studios original content which will only be broadcast on their platforms. *The Queen's*

Gambit, *Stranger Things* and *La casa de papel* are some of my most favourite original content that has kept me a Netflix subscriber, and likely will for the foreseeable future if they continue to invest like they are currently. In the first quarter of 2021, Netflix confirmed that it was planning and on track to spend $17 billion on original content that year, up from $11.8 billion in 2020 (Netflix, 2021a).

So, how did Netflix move through their first three acts so successfully, whilst others have failed? Well, it comes down to the culture of innovation they have fostered (Netflix, 2021b). Patty McCord was the leader of the human resources function within Netflix for fourteen years and published a book titled *Powerful: Building a culture of freedom and responsibility*, which provided in-depth insights into the culture at Netflix (McCord, 2018). This insight, coupled with the infamous 'Netflix Culture Deck' (Netflix, 2009) which Sheryl Sandberg, the Facebook Chief Operating Officer said was 'the most important document to ever to come of the Valley', has given us stunning levels of insight into the inside workings of the company (Shontell, 2013).

Netflix encourage their employees to '*make decisions based on the long term*', which we know is good for innovation, as attention switches from the demands of meeting quarterly targets. Netflix also promote '*curiosity*' and '*innovation*' as core values within their teams, demanding that *people say what they think*, even when it's uncomfortable, as well as asking each employee to create new ideas, *re-conceptualize issues to discover solutions*, and *challenge the prevailing assumptions*. One great example of challenging the status quo relates to the implementation of the 'download' function, so users can download content to watch offline. The idea was first opposed by Hastings, but a team of researchers from within Netflix tested it with customers and proved its value, and Hastings was quick to agree to its implementation (and I for one am grateful) – the key here is that the culture of Netflix enabled employees to work on an idea that had originally been dismissed, and *the team was comfortable to act in the company's best interest, not the highest-paid individual's* (Koss, 2020).

At Netflix, they also spend time *reducing bureaucracy* and *freeing up their teams from process*, which is proven to stifle innovation efforts (Anthony et al, 2019). And finally, you can also see many cases of people within Netflix making mistakes or missteps when it comes to innovation, and the company very publicly highlights that those *mistakes are not fatal to someone's career* at Netflix (Hastings and Meyer, 2020).

The fourth act will almost certainly see the need for another shift, and it will be very interesting to watch as the current biggest content creators Amazon, Apple, Hulu, Netflix, etc, battle it out. Whoever has a culture of innovation and the willingness to adapt their business model is sure to steal a march on their competition once again.

Outcome bias

Just as Blockbuster fell into the trap of believing in their own success, so did Nokia. As had Kodak, and many more famous names. These beloved giants of industry all passed the same way. They thought that what made them successful would keep them successful, and that their great work thus far would continue to sustain their businesses. They *ignored the luck and good fortune that had come their way* (which is needed in any successful venture) and they considered themselves smarter than the rest. The trap they fell into was that of *outcome bias*. It's a bias which makes us blind and stops us from innovation or changing, and it's all too common. So, if you want a culture of innovation you have to battle this as hard as you can.

So, what happened to Nokia? Well, the case study of Nokia surprised me as it was a company founded in 1865 as a paper mill. And since its inception it went through various innovation cycles and focused on industries such as paper, rubber, tyre, televisions and lately mobile phones. It clearly had a culture of innovation and changing in the face of new headwinds and trends, much like we just saw with Netflix. However, as it rose to dominance since the launch of its first telecommunications devices in the early 1990s, becoming the top-selling mobile phone provider in 1998, with Blackberry, Samsung and Apple way behind in the phone stakes, things changed.

As Nokia dominated and innovated its way through history, introducing the first camera phone in 2003, and constantly improving its technology year in and year out, the iPhone from Apple launched in 2007. At this point, Nokia had around a 50 per cent market share of all mobile phones sold globally, and Apple was a pimple on an elephant's bottom in terms of market share (Statista Research Department, 2013). Now, we will never know if this fable is true, and I have only heard it recanted third hand, but there is a story that a group of Nokia executives were out at dinner one night discussing business, and in particular discussing their competitors; Blackberry was their most pressing concern, especially amongst business users. But there was indeed an elephant in the room, which was Apple and the iPhone. The strange thing was that at this dinner the executives around the table allegedly all had an iPhone in their pockets, and were using it as their personal phone, but they all made a similar comment to that of the Blockbuster CEO, in that Apple just wasn't on their competitive radar.

Alas, they were either in denial or falling into the trap of outcome bias, especially as Nokia was spending $5.7 billion on research and development of mobile phone technology on an annual basis with a level of consistency – there was no way they couldn't continue being successful (Nokia, 2007). However, as you know, the tables had turned and Nokia failed to innovate its product and anticipate customer needs, and its market share dwindled from just under the 50 per cent mark down to only 3 per cent in a matter of less than five years (Statista Research Department, 2013). In 2014 Nokia sold its mobile phone division to Microsoft, and it has made a somewhat muted comeback since.

So, what can you do practically to avoid complacency and outcome bias from creeping in and having these devastating consequences? You could try any combination of the following:

- *Make decisions based upon leading indicators* (indicators and data points that predict the future). Many companies look at key performance indicators and data points that tell a story of the past, i.e. how many customers you have, or how much revenue you have generated. And, whilst these are fine metrics, they are limited in their outlook to the future. Instead, *consider a set of leading indicators that can help you identify what will happen in the future*, i.e. customer satisfaction (if it drops, you should soon expect to lose customers) and the R-number (the rate of any disease's ability to spread – if its above 1.0 then we can expect exponential growth of a disease, as we have all learnt during the Covid-19 crisis).

- Constantly *test alternative hypotheses* (don't stay faithful to your existing way of doing business, as it may not be future proof) so you stay ahead of the curve. *Set time aside* for these activities, build it into your strategic planning process.

- Try to *analyse why things happened* in your business, to *see if luck played a part* (it most certainly did) and thus openly and honestly review business practices through a very clear lens. Once you know why things happened and what caused the outcomes, you will be better placed to make enhanced decisions.

- *When faced without a challenge, make one up*. My final piece of advice here is based upon research by the *British Medical Journal*, which showed that people who retire at the age of 55 are 89 per cent more likely to die in the following ten years than those who retire at 65 years old. Humans are hardwired to face challenges, and the same can go for companies. If everything looks good in your company, it's probably the right time to create some challenges – make them up if they don't exist (Tsai et al, 2005).

The LEGO Group – the ultimate battler

As I alluded to, you have to battle outcome bias and force yourself to change if it's not coming naturally. And here is where your culture is vital. The good news is that you can build this type of innovation culture by focusing on it deliberately and in a sustained manner.

As we saw with Nokia, they had it – pivoting from paper to phone – but then they lost it, as they were not laser-focused on it. It is a constant game; you need to have consistency as you do when brushing your teeth, or working out at the gym. Consistent application wins.

However, one company is a shining light of an innovative culture, and we can find them headquartered in a small town called Billund in Denmark. That company is The LEGO Group, one of the most remarkable companies in the world.

One of my favourite photos I like to show my students and audiences, when speaking on this topic, is a picture of four wooden toys. It is a picture of a duck on wheels, a car, a fire engine and a wooden yoyo. These were toys produced in Denmark during the 1930s by, you guessed it, The LEGO Group. The LEGO Group started off its life as a carpentry workshop, and many of these first wooden toys are now collectors' pieces and fetch great prices. But, isn't it strange that a company we associate with bricks actually started its life as a carpentry workshop? The image of four wooden toys can be quite surprising when you learn the name of the company behind it.

After the Second World War, in the late 1940s, the use of plastics became prevalent in manufacturing and The LEGO Group purchased plastic injection moulding equipment. In 1949 production of the first LEGO bricks began, and it didn't get off to a good start – with wooden toys continuing to be favoured. But the team continued pressing ahead with both business lines. Twenty years later, in the late 1960s, LEGO bricks were the talk of the town and the company was producing millions of sets of bricks. In 1968

The LEGO Group even opened its first LEGOLAND theme park in its hometown of Billund, which remains open to this day, albeit on an even grander scale as the company continued to grow.

From the 1970s through to the 1990s The LEGO Group continued to innovate, mostly focused on product innovation: making the blocks stronger, adding a few new components to the sets, and creating the Duplo range of products for young children. The teams at The LEGO Group had a culture of innovation through testing, listening to customers, and seeking feedback in order to make wonderful products that consumers loved.

But then, in the 1990s The LEGO Group hit a bump in the road. Many of the old guard colleagues had retired and been replaced with new young designers – who even got rid of the Duplo brand at one point – and many parts of The LEGO Group business (such as manufacturing) were moved to third-parties who were far removed from the day-to-day workings of The LEGO Group and their customers. Neither the new hires, nor the third parties, knew the business of The LEGO Group nor their unique culture of innovation and invention.

For new hires, their onboarding into the company wasn't as it should have been: they didn't spend time getting to know the history of The LEGO Group or its culture, and they were not close to the customers who were the lifeblood of the company, the collectors and enthusiasts. Customers rebelled and asked for the classic designs to come back, but the new employees were not listening, and this cumulated in 1998 with The LEGO Group posting its first-ever loss of £23 million. Things didn't get much better for the next few years as The LEGO Group stumbled along, seemingly having lost its culture and innovation capabilities. In 2004 the group lost £174 million (The LEGO Group, 2004), and the CEO resigned.

A new CEO, Jørgen Vig Knudstorp, joined in 2004 and the Duplo brand was re-instated, manufacturing was moved back in house, and bit by bit The LEGO Group started to come back to life. Once again The LEGO Group focused on building the culture, listened to customers, sought feedback and gave everyone within the company a voice. The LEGO Group began signing licence agreements with large brands and began to create new products like board games with LEGO Ninjago and LEGO Power Miners, two notable successes (BCG, 2017). In 2012, *The LEGO Story*, a short film, was released, and it was followed in 2014 by a joint project with Warner Bros titled *The LEGO Movie*. We have since seen *The LEGO Batman Movie* and a huge range of new licence agreements including a couple of my personal favourite LEGO sets, those of *Friends* and *Stranger Things*.

So, how did The LEGO Group turn it around and rethink its business model? Well, remember Jørgen Vig Knudstorp, the CEO that had joined at The LEGO Group's lowest ebb in 2004? Vig Knudstorp had decreed that the company had become arrogant and had detached itself from its customers. He identified that the success The LEGO Group had experienced had resulted in a very singular culture. So, he relentlessly focused on changing the culture and ensured that The LEGO Group *prioritized its mission and vision to help children learn systematic, creative problem solving* (Davis, 2017). Loren Shuster, the Chief People Officer and Head of Corporate Affairs at The LEGO Group, told me that they focused once more on 'The LEGO idea paper', an internal document written by the founding family, which described their belief that 'children are our role models'. With a renewed focus on this, and its mission, The LEGO Group moved towards its core culture once again: *listening to its customers*, as it did in the 1970s so successfully. And, to this day, Loren says that The LEGO Group continues to 'engage with [customers] on a very regular basis, to get a sense of what is important to them and how they relate to the product or experience'. The LEGO Group has mastered the art of understanding what it is that customers are telling the company, even when they are children.

As Vig Knudstorp stabilized The LEGO Group, more artistic licence became possible: in 2008 they *launched a crowdsourcing platform called LEGO IDEAS*, to receive feedback from the market. They were one of the first companies to make this bold move. This solicitation of public feedback sits well alongside their Danish roots as a company, with The LEGO Group adopting 'a *non-hierarchical structure*, that enables a very low power distance' to be in place, coupled with the fact that '*leadership is for everyone*' which means all creative and innovative ideas are listened to and treated the same way. Loren says, in simplified terms, that 'within The LEGO Group we have our creative process called the "LEGO Development Process", and we have very diverse groups of people in these, engaged in exploration, selection and decision making. There is *not one person alone who can say "no" to an idea*'.

The culture of innovation is engrained in the business, and their corporate values, which include 'imagination, creativity, fun, learning, caring and quality', help drive this culture forwards. They also work against the backdrop of '65–70 per cent of sales each year coming from products that had been launched in that year' so there is pressure from their customers in that regard, not counting the fact that their youngest user group (children) 'often grow out of a particular LEGO product set, usually within five to eight years, which is unlike banking where customers may keep their bank account for their life'.

Vig Knudstorp also brought back much of the third-party activity. And, today, 'The LEGO Group manufactures 100 per cent of their products internally, and use c. 96 per cent of components from in-house sources' – meaning they can control and ensure quality, and 'fully express and realize the innovative ideas of the designers'.

Interestingly, in 2015 when Vig Knudstorp presented The LEGO Group's financial results (the tenth consecutive year of profits) he took the time to speak to his management team. After he praised them for their record performance, which was profits higher than the next three competitors combined, he asked them a question. He asked them if The LEGO Group was playing and competing in the toy market after all. What he meant, and where his question probed, was the need to *redefine not only their business model but also the market*. He asked the management team to consider what a child would buy if it wasn't a LEGO toy. The answer was not a Megablocks or a Fisherprice, it was more likely to be a Playstation or an iPhone, and thus, culturally their transformation had moved full circle, they were once again innovating, just as they had done when they moved from wooden toys to plastic blocks. By avoiding the outcome bias trap they fell into in the late 1990s they continued to expand: The LEGO Group had moved out of its lane (O'Connell, 2009).

The LEGO Group entered the education market with LEGO Education, wonderful toy sets to teach coding and other relevant skills to youngsters in a playful way. They also entered the business market, and I use LEGO Serious Play in culture workshops for various challenges. Outside the office, I walk around in some wonderful Adidas Ultraboost DNA x LEGO Plates trainers which were released in 2021. Since the trainers launched, new pairs and new innovative designs incorporating physical LEGO bricks into the shoes are being released on a seemingly monthly basis – I will have to 'borrow' my parents' credit card again!

Loren confirmed to me what I suspected, that 'The LEGO Group brand is so much wider than just a toy company; it is an ecosystem of experiences (beyond children's play sets, with adults deeply engaged too), and an entertainment company, as our products are surrounded by content that creates narrative, context and storytelling, for the play experience to be enriched and appreciated.' And that is quite some move for a company that started out in carpentry, with wooden toys.

The LEGO fan in me lives on.

It's your choice

Whilst we are living the Fourth Industrial Revolution, you have a choice. You can wait to be eaten by a competitor and fall into irrelevance. As the cartoons in the business press often say, and I paraphrase here, 'instead of taking a risk on something new, let's be sure to play safe by failing to try anything risky, and guaranteeing our decline into obsolescence'. This light-hearted joke is deadly serious – you really can become irrelevant. As I say, '*If you don't take risks, you also take a risk.*'

Or, you can of course take steps to continue innovating. If you choose to rethink your business model and make brave decisions about what your products are, the markets you serve and how you do that you will be well placed.

Nike put it best when they founded the company. They set out ten business principles, ten key characteristics and things that culturally they wanted Nike to be like. The first principle was the most important, and it was '*Our business is change*'. Since its founding, Nike has iterated on the ten business principles and now calls them 'eleven maxims', which do exactly the same job as the original ten, setting out the way of operating and the culture of the company. In first place is, you guessed it, '*It's in our nature to innovate*' (Connell-Waite, 2014).

Let that be a lesson to all of us. Our culture has to be receptive to change, and we have to be aware that what we do today won't necessarily lead us to glory in the future. It is vital we avoid outcome bias. The competition is not staying in its lane any longer and attacks are coming from all angles. So, it is imperative that you have a culture that is receptive to rethinking your business model.

QUESTIONS FOR REFLECTION

- How much have you rethought your business model in the past five years?
- How much will you rethink your business model in the next five years?
- What business principles do you have, like Nike, that suggest that your business is change?
- Thinking like LEGO, who are your expanded list of competitors, as well as new clients?
- How do you currently scan the market for potential disruptions and changes?
- What do you do to fight outcome bias within your company?
- Which chunk of your existing business will you start now to cannibalize for your longer-term success?

The next chapter will cover our second principle: creating creativity with constraints. Many businesses fail to innovate in the manner they need because they throw too many resources and too much money at the problem, and find themselves stagnating. I will set out the case for creating innovation by imposing constraints on your innovation efforts, and forcing your teams to ideate fast, improving and polishing later.

03

Create creativity with constraints

A need or problem encourages creative efforts to meet the need or solve the problem. Necessity is the mother of invention.

PLATO

In this chapter we are going to discuss how imposing constraints can actually strengthen your culture of innovation and lead you to more success. We will see that constraints often breed creativity, and the reverse is true when you have unlimited time and resources: you often get sub-optimal outcomes.

We will learn that resources are simply not the differentiator, and that a culture of constraint – especially self-imposed constraint – can lead to thriving companies, and plenty of innovation. The demand for resources, time and budget is always limitless within companies and this leads to excuses for poor performance, delays in delivery and general slippage in the innovation process. There are always justifications and reasons for the demands. Nothing is ever perfect or finished and everything can always be improved. But the key, when innovating, is to start and deliver something (the minimum viable product) despite its imperfections – they can always be enhanced at a later stage.

When you find yourself with a need or a necessity then innovation is likely to follow.

Huge amounts of research and development spending

As we saw in the previous chapter, Nokia, the darling of the telecommunications industry, was spending huge sums of money on research and development, which Apple, the creators of the iPhone, just could not afford to do. Or, did not want to do.

It was a scenario that saw Nokia invest another $3.9 billion in the financial year for 2010 (on top of the tens of billions they had spent in previous years), with little Apple spending only $800 million, and other competitors like HTC spending under $500 million (Scott, 2011). And, as we know, the results were quite stark.

Nokia certainly did not get the bang for their buck that they desperately needed, and their just under 50 per cent market share eroded to 3 per cent a few years later, as Apple, HTC, Samsung et al. took off to the moon in terms of smartphone dominance (Lee, 2013). Why was this the case?

It's not about how much you spend

So, it really *isn't about how much you spend* or invest in research and development activities. Of course, having money to spend can be an advantage, and done well, fantastic outcomes can and do occur. However, the *more important factor is how you spend* the money as opposed to just spending great quantities of money. In the introduction we saw that you do need to have a strong strategy for your innovation efforts, but the *cultural aspect and mental process of making these decisions* is even more valuable.

If you cannot afford, or – even better – don't want to spend as much money on research and development as your competitors then you must look for different angles and different ways to undertake your research and development efforts.

When you are cooking, and the recipe calls for an ultra-expensive ingredient that you can only buy in a 1kg bag, yet you only need 5g for the recipe, what do you do? Do you spend the money knowing that you are going to waste nearly the whole bag of product, or do you search for a more fitting solution: experimenting and trying a substitute ingredient instead?

There are numerous examples of companies spending their money in different ways, using different tactics, or substitutes, and getting great results. The most famous story in recent times comes from the world of sports. And this story in particular was so inspiring and the success was so unimaginable that the story was turned into a film staring Brad Pitt.

Of course, I am referencing *Moneyball*. It was released in 2011, bringing to life one of the most incredible sporting stories related to culture ever seen. The film was based upon a 2003 book with the same title by Michael Lewis.

In both the book and the film, the story centres upon the Oakland Athletics baseball team and their 2002 season. They were a team led by their general manager, Billy Beane (Brad Pitt) and their assistant general manager Peter Brand (Jonah Hill), who was an economics graduate with a keen eye for data.

The Oakland Athletics baseball team, it is fair to say, *had no history of winning and one of the smallest budgets* in the league. They had lost their best players during the course of the season's break and needed to rebuild the team. Normal practice was to ask the scouts to find the best players they could using their eyes and build a team using every last cent in their (limited) budget. However, Billy and Peter had different ideas, and wanted to exploit the use of data to try and maximize their investments. They spent their money in large part on data, and they *looked for patterns that were non-traditional*, avoiding the use of the most popular metrics used in the early 2000s and *interrogating massive lakes of data that were previously unused* in order to try and find hidden gems. They started to use Sabermetrics, such as the 'On base percentage', excluding when they reach the base thanks to an opposition error or the fielding team's choice (i.e. they want the base move). They also looked at things like the 'On base plus slugging' metric, which considers how powerful a batter is. These two metrics required the analytics team to take various data points and crunch them to come to the final result. Previously, teams just looked at the most basic of data and didn't use advanced analytic techniques to mine the data points for insight. In the case of Oakland Athletics, put simply, they were being forced, because of financial constraint, to use different tactics, substitute ingredients and *spend their money differently*.

They faced uphill battles with their scouting network. Many maintained that the scout's eye was more important than the data. But then who wouldn't protect their own job, if they were not willing to change their own lane for the good of their career? And they faced an uphill battle with Art Howe, who was the Oakland Athletics manager on the field, the one who picks the team and executes the game strategy.

Suffice to say, their methods worked – otherwise the story would likely not be a feature-length film. Little by little, Billy and Peter built the team they wanted and the team brought as much success as could be imagined in most people's wildest dreams. Though they didn't win the World Series of baseball, they out-batted their rivals and punched above their weight for the size of their budget. They broke records along the way, like twenty consecutive wins, which was unheard of – and, they had sustained success in their division.

At a fork in the road, Billy was offered the chance to move role and join the Boston Red Sox. He was offered the chance to implement his systems in that company, but he declined – despite supposedly being offered the highest ever general manager salary in sports history. He had proven that a constraint in budget, when the culture was right and thinking outside the box prevailed, could lead to success.

The model Billy and Peter created was then subject to much copying, as is usual with innovations. However, they were the first, and rightly have the credit. Indeed, their model was so successful that the owner of the Boston Red Sox, John W Henry, implemented it – without Billy – in his organization and broke an 86-year wait for a World Series win for the Boston Red Sox in 2004.

John W Henry then bought Liverpool Football Club in the UK in 2010 and, taking the principles of constraint and creativity he had successfully implemented, put them in place in his new football club. Since he has owned the club, they have gone on to great success, breaking a 36-year wait for the Premier League, and also winning the Champions League.

As more and more companies, and in this example sports clubs, replicate and copy the route to innovation, this shows that you have to always challenge yourself to become ever more creative.

Fortunately, the constraint need not be restricted only to financial aspects.

It's often about the level of urgency

I was fortunate enough to be travelling in the summer of 2021 and found myself passing through the British Airways lounge at Heathrow Airport, which is located in Terminal 5.

As you enter you are given a 'code of the day' by the reception staff. I will explain what this code is used for later on. You can sit down wherever you please, enjoy the comfy chairs and service, recharge your mobile devices, and stare out of the window onto the tarmac of the airport – watching the (few) planes go by to your heart's content.

The interesting thing, given the onset of Covid-19 and the new practices and procedures put in place to combat the spread of the disease, is that there is no longer a buffet selection of food and drink. This is obviously a logical and useful strategy in combatting the spread of the Covid-19 virus. However, tummies do rumble and people usually enjoy a pre-flight glass of champagne or a snack or sandwich. The buffet has been replaced with a little sticker on your table, with a table number and QR code. Rows and rows of buffet tables have been replaced with a sticker.

Visitors are instructed to scan the QR code of their table by opening their mobile phone camera and pointing it at the QR code. Once you have done this, a message appears on the top of your screen inviting you to access a website. When you click to enter the website, you are taken to the landing page which asks for your name, and the 'code of the day' which is a secret phrase used by those visiting the lounge to ensure some level of safety that the system is not abused by non-visitors, and the table number (which is pre-populated based on the QR code).

Once you have logged in, which takes all of two seconds to do since you have scanned the QR code, you are taken to a menu. And it is in this menu you can order food and drink until your stomach is sufficiently full. Once you place your order with a simple click of a button, the clear user interface allows you to check the status of your order and you need only wait a few minutes before your food and drink is brought to you by the team of professionals in the lounge.

Now, there have been very few industries as hard hit as the aviation industry during the Covid-19 pandemic, and it has necessitated that companies innovate and change to meet the prevailing needs of customers, and regulatory requirements imposed upon them. What caught my attention was a little footnote at the bottom of the website which reads 'Copyright 2020, all rights reserved – Hangar 51 – IAG'.

Now, I have heard before of IAG. It stands for International Airlines Group and is the corporate parent company for British Airways, Iberia, Aer Lingus, Iberia Express, Vueling, Level IAG Cargo and IAG Loyalty. So, I wasn't surprised to see the letters IAG after the copyright claim. However, the words Hangar 51 were a little newer to me, so I set off to research what this was.

As it turns out, Hangar 51 is the group of people tasked with leading digital transformation for the IAG group of companies. And, Hangar 51 has a very interesting story behind it, in terms of the culture of innovation it brings to the party.

Hangar 51 has a stated mission to 'inspire, transform and innovate with IAG and the travel industry' (Hangar 51, 2020). They are looking to 'demonstrate the art of the possible using emerging technologies and techniques' and their approach has many spokes to it. They fund, support and scale start-up companies and help them to partner with the IAG branded companies, giving them access to over one hundred million passengers each year.

Since their launch in 2017, Hangar 51 has been successful for IAG. Very successful in fact. Not only have they quickly supported the rollout of the very elegant food ordering system powered by an app in the lounge of British Airways at Terminal 5, but they have been ranked number one out of sixty-six global airline groups for digital transformation by Frost and Sullivan (2019) and solutions coming out of the project have saved over £90 million in costs through automation, and helped implement a truly digital mindset throughout the group with Hangar 51 screening over 1,700 technologies since it launched (Hangar 51, 2020).

Whilst they invest in start-ups, perhaps their biggest success has been the Hangar 51 Accelerator. And, it is in this accelerator that constraints create creativity. *When a start-up or scale-up is accepted into the Hangar 51 Accelerator programme they have just ten weeks to access real-world environments*, be that the planes, the data, the lounges, the customers, the pilots and crew, and work with a range of Hangar 51 staff and industry experts to develop and produce their product or prototype.

Ten weeks! Just ten weeks to finesse a business, a new idea, a completely new concept. Talk about pressure and constraint. At the end of the ten weeks the company has to present the solution or product to the senior management of IAG at a 'Demo Day' and there the decision is made to invest, continue or discontinue with the project.

And, well, it does seem that the *pressure cooker environment* and constraint of having just ten weeks to perfect your pitch works. To date, sixty companies have successfully come out the other side of the Hangar 51 Accelerator programme and their solutions are flying the skies as we speak.

Some of their successes, such as Airboard, which offers real-time digital queues that appear on your mobile phone, and avoids the need for people to physically queue in this socially distanced world, make our lives so much easier and safer.

Others, like BagsID, process images of passenger luggage and remove the need for paper tags and stickers to be placed on the bags. Some like to collect the stickers on their bags and wear them as a sign of frequent flying, but reducing friction in the process and innovating on technology is always welcome in an environment that deals with millions of pieces of luggage.

Climatetrade helps the airlines to offset their carbon footprint by investing in green projects, which are tracked using blockchain. And, the list goes on and on. Many successes have come out of this super-constrained approach to innovation, and no doubt the innovative solutions are helping to soften the extremely hard blow the aviation industry faces at the time of writing.

Other pressure cookers

This tactic of creating urgency seems to herald success not just for IAG but also for many others, irrespective of industry.

In accelerators or pressure cookers around the world, people are innovating at a wonderful pace, which is so vital in this, the Fourth Industrial Revolution. When companies are built for speed, and the culture mandates it, it is more likely than not that they will outpace and win versus those who are slow and set in their ways.

Bayer is one of the largest pharmaceutical companies in the world, based in Leverkusen in Germany. They were founded in 1863, making them over 150 years old, certainly outliving the average company lifespan curve. They have grown from humble beginnings to now employing over 100,000 colleagues worldwide (as of 2019) and report profits of over $4 billion (again in 2019), on revenues just shy of $44 billion (Bayer, 2020).

MasterCard is in the payments business. They are a company based in O'Fallon in the United States and have been around since 1966, making them fifty-five years old at the time of writing. Their products are used by millions around the world and their 2020 profits were over $6.4 billion, aided by their band of 21,000 colleagues (Mastercard, 2019).

Both of these firms display very similar cultural traits, despite their differences in size and industry. They too have built a culture of innovation, by using constraints to create creativity – much like IAG and Hangar 51. Let us have a look inside their pressure cookers.

Bayer has an accelerator called Grant4Apps, which they launched in 2013 and which now operates out of 35 different countries worldwide. In this accelerator the most promising start-ups in the field of digital health technology get to join. They receive €50,000 and are locked up in a Bayer campus for three months. Not quite as urgent as with Hangar 51, but given most advances in the world of pharmaceuticals take ten or twenty years, quite constrained. In similar fashion to Hangar 51, the participants have access to the top leaders of Bayer and are advised on a weekly basis about their progress and product development. As well as the start-ups taking advantage of the money and access to develop wonderful products, the team at Bayer also wins by this arrangement. Not only can they access first-hand new technologies and innovations and invest or incorporate them into their company, the staff are learning alongside those in the start-ups about how to innovate, how to have speed, and they perceive that the learning has trickled down across the whole company. Meaning even those colleagues who are not directly involved in the Grant4Apps programme learn from the innovation that is ongoing, and the benefits of the accelerator are much wider than the immediate ones.

CarePay is one of my personal favourite innovations coming out of the Grant4Apps programme as they spent their time in the Grants4Apps accelerator programme developing a health benefit wallet to operate on mobile phones. They launched in Kenya, and are based in Nigeria and Tanzania. Patients are linked, by mobile phone, directly with their insurance company and the doctors. So, CarePay can ensure that providers get their claims for insurance approved fast and without bureaucracy, which means patients get faster treatments, and insurance companies have real-time, clear visibility of liabilities. It is a win–win–win scenario for all involved, and in 2021 over 4.7 million people were connected to the platform, with growth continuing as more doctors and healthcare providers get onboard daily, offering patients the widest possible choice of services (CarePay, 2021).

It isn't just me who took notice of CarePay and the benefits it is bringing to society; in 2018 it garnered recognition from the World Economic Forum, and, in 2019 won the SwissRe Entrepreneurs for Resilience Award, which focuses on solutions that promote better healthcare for households in low-income areas.

MasterCard launched MasterCard Labs in 2010. This is MasterCard's pressure cooker, with the aim of rapidly innovating and bringing innovative payment solutions to the forefront. They too operate globally, with hubs around the world, and take start-ups through a similar programme to what we have seen in Hangar 51 and Grants4Apps. The MasterCard Labs programme has been responsible for QkR (amongst other innovations), which is a product for schools that launched first in Australia. QkR is a mobile payment app that helps parents and students order lunch at schools or other school items such as uniforms, textbooks or merchandise. The app reduces the burden on school administrators and accountants, the parents have full visibility of spending, and students learn about finance without having to carry significant sums of cash to school.

As part of their MasterCard Labs, MasterCard have also *developed an 'innovation express' methodology which sees very intense 48-hour 'developer-thon' periods* of innovation. Now we are talking about a much smaller time period than three months in Grant4Apps and ten weeks in Hangar 51. They have used this intense 48-hour period to innovate at speed with their customers, corporate clients, partners and participants in the MasterCard Labs main programme. As well as this, the innovation express format has been used at universities with students and they have rolled out competitions to colleagues across MasterCard globally so all staff can have their say in idea generation and solution creation. Later, we will touch more on the benefits of these kinds of approaches when casting the net wide and seeking 'the wisdom of the crowd'.

SpaceX

SpaceX was founded in 2002, and unless you have been sleeping in a cave for the past nineteen years you will have heard of this rocket manufacturer based in Hawthorne, United States and founded by Elon Musk, one of the most prominent inventors, visionaries and entrepreneurs of the twenty-first century.

SpaceX was founded by Musk with the mission of reducing the cost of space transport in order to enable the colonization of Mars, so that we humans could become a multi-planetary species. Whilst SpaceX is a fantastic study of leadership (both good and bad) and culture (which we will touch upon in more depth in the next chapter) it is also the backdrop to a curious case of constraints helping to create creativity.

In this case, *Musk himself was the constraint*, and continues to be the constraint. Musk is a firm believer that the human species needs to become multi-planetary in order to survive and thrive in the future, and he is convinced that humans need a back-up to planet Earth. So, he set out on perhaps his most ambitious project yet, despite Tesla, Neuralink and The Boring Company all promising to solve huge challenges for us Earth-dwelling individuals in the way of creating sustainable transport and energy, obtained through electric vehicles, and in the case of Tesla, through solar power. Nuralink is on a mission to wirelessly connect the brain to the digital world, with the connection with our smartphones first on the list. And, finally, The Boring Company – which is such a great name for a company that makes holes in the ground – aims to solve traffic congestion by having a series of underground tunnels that allow riders to travel at speeds of up to 150mph without any traffic jams or crashes.

SpaceX clearly wants to get people to Mars – despite it being 140 million miles away, or 225 million kilometres. What a great ambition! Mars is one of Earth's closest habitable neighbours as it has sunlight and the atmosphere is conducive to growing plants, there is gravity (though it is just 38 per cent of that on Earth) and the days mirror fairly well those of Earth, at 24 hours and 37 minutes in length.

So, why is Elon Musk himself the constraint? Well, he is the constraint not only because he fears that *the window of opportunity to reach Mars may not be open forever* (i.e. we have just a number of years to achieve this feat before it is too late) and it may be impossible due to changing conditions, but also that *Musk's own lifetime is finite*, and this is a mission he wants to achieve personally.

In addition to Musk pushing for speed, there has also been *a significant financial constraint* at SpaceX. As detailed in Eric Berger's insightful book, *Liftoff: Elon Musk and the desperate early days that launched SpaceX* (2021), SpaceX was funded by Musk, who had nothing like the money that their competitors had, having committed to invest around $100 million into SpaceX. Kistler Aerospace, an established competitor, went bankrupt around the same time (2003) with debts of $600 million and assets of just $6 million, and this was a company 'that didn't even get out of bed for contracts worth less than $10 million'. Others, such as Lockheed and Boeing's joint venture, United Launch Alliance, received funding from the government to the tune of around $1 billion per year, and then extra money for rocket launches – a completely different financial situation to that which Musk and SpaceX faced (Berger, 2021).

So, with Musk's own finite lifespan, the window of opportunity closing on the chance to become a multi-planetary species and the fact that their endeavours were funded by just one individual who had limited money and not by big, juicy government contracts, SpaceX had their own pressure cooker and constraints well defined.

These constraints contributed to the first Falcon 1 launch attempt coming only three years and ten months after the founding of the company – just imagine for a second the sheer engineering and complexity involved in designing a rocket capable of launching to space from scratch with limited resources. This was a huge achievement, and despite the rocket not successfully completing the desired mission, they kept going and the team at SpaceX first reached space only a year later, just four years and ten months after the launch of the company. Even more impressive was that they made orbit in six years and four months, and keep going from strength to strength, thanks to their impressive culture of constraints breeding creativity.

And, just like rocket engines, when you combine the level of urgency with a lack of money you often get explosive innovation.

The rise of Uber

We have seen that large corporates such as IAG and Bayer can innovate at scale, and can quickly use some of the techniques we have seen (create a pressure cooker environment, have a short period of time, and little funding). Innovation is not limited to any population, and that is an important message. Our brains often default to the fact that innovation is most prolific in start-ups. And, this default position is for good reason; everyone loves the story of a small company taking on the big players and it is true they have many advantages related to being small. With all employees being *hyperconnected* to one another, they have *huge amounts of accountability* within these companies as there is no place to hide in a team of ten people who know your every move, they often gear the high levels of risk which innovation thrives upon to reward, and employees are *rewarded like Kings and Queens* when things go well. These three advantages are very relevant.

That said, start-ups of course face a whole set of other challenges when it comes to innovation. Not least is a lack of funding and the absolutely desperate need to innovate and iterate their way to a market and then sustain success by way of profits and positive cash flow. These constraints are arguably much more powerful than the advantages that help them to innovate rapidly.

Uber is the brainchild of Travis Kalanick and Garrett Camp, and was an idea formed in 2008 when Camp grew frustrated with the lack of taxis in his city of San Francisco. Camp tried to bend the ear of Kalanick but wasn't successful in starting Uber until one night in Paris, France when they couldn't find a taxi to take them home and the frustration grew; they knew they were onto something. The two friends set out to develop a mobile app that would let people hail rides at the click of a button, from their own smartphones. And in 2009 they launched a beta version of the app in San Francisco – with its first user taking a trip in an Uber in 2010 (Uber, 2021).

Things accelerated from there, much like an Uber driver coming down the motorway. By the end of 2015 their app had spread and one billion trips had been completed just five and a half years after the first (Kokalitcheva, 2015). The company branched off into food delivery, self-driving vehicle pilots, freight delivery, and by June 2018 had connected people over 10 billion times (Dickey, 2018). The growth was exponential at this stage.

Just ten years after its founding, on 9 May 2019, the company went public. Today, in November of 2021, Uber is valued at over \$87 billion, making it a top 200 company in the world by market capitalization, i.e. value of the business (Yahoo Finance, 2021b).

This sounds like a great business and one that had headwinds behind it and everything went smoothly, but the real story is anything but smooth. So, how did Uber take on the taxi industry and win?

Well, their size both helped and hindered them initially. Starting out, and going through a hyper growth phase meant that they were always *short on cash*, this was constraint number one. Constraint number two was that they *faced huge regulatory challenges* to launching in cities around the United States, and the incumbent taxi companies complained to politicians, who were lobbied by trade unions – all of which cumulated in Uber being one of the most hated companies in cities upon their launch.

These two challenges spurred Uber onto massive growth. First, the fact that Uber had far fewer resources in terms of finance, people and cars (they didn't have any ownership of the cars that were meant to transport customers across towns and cities) actually helped them; they realized very quickly that if they didn't have a sense of urgency they wouldn't have any company as no income would mean no venture capital funds and a quick retreat from the market. The incumbent taxi firms, with all of their cash, their monopolies and their resources in terms of drivers and cars fell into the trap described in the previous chapter about outcome bias. They couldn't see the attack and changing business model coming, and didn't want to appreciate its looming impacts – they chose to ignore the competition and hope that it went away, despite the fact they were in pole position to seize the day.

Equally, when it came to the legislative barriers and hurdles put up to Uber in each city they went to, fuelled by the same taxi companies that chose to protect their business through legislation, lawyers and courts rather than innovate and enhance their product, Uber had to act fast. Uber was not sitting on a pile of cash and could not wait it out; they had the urgency of a commercial business that needed solutions fast in order to survive.

So, these two constraints *forced Uber to move, and move fast*. That is what they did. They took the approach that building scale fast was necessary and set out on this path with laser focus. Step by step they moved from city to city, slowly dominating the ride-hailing industry. As of 2021, it is estimated that Uber accounts for 69 per cent of all ride hailing in the United States – that is a two-thirds market share, in ten years (Burgueño Salas, 2021)!

Now, it is true that Uber hasn't had a smooth ride. The legislative and regulatory constraints thrown in their way were tough, and coupled with the pressure from trade unions and police officers, starting up in new cities wasn't easy. As Mike Isaac described in his book *Super Pumped*, Uber had a clear strategy for overcoming these challenges – and their answer was speed (Isaac, 2019).

In 2014 Uber launched in Portland. They had been in discussions for a number of months with the local law makers and politicians, explaining the Uber concept and the benefits it would bring to citizens of Portland to have a safe, secure, cheap and convenient method of transport. The transportation officials pushed back, and said that ride-hailing laws hadn't been written just yet and Uber would have to wait for their grand launch. Uber had other plans; with dwindling cash as always a problem, they took the approach of launching their offering and suffering any consequences at a later date.

Kalanick approved the launch of the service in Portland, and with an army of agents on the ground, drivers, being offered $500 cash bonuses after their first customer, were rapidly signed up and customers were offered free ride codes, handed out like newspapers at a train station. The strategy was to launch, and get large enough rapidly, so that customers and drivers would then complain to their local politicians if the transport authorities or local law makers put further blocks in the way of Uber.

This strategy worked, and Uber grew. However, in 2017 Uber was exposed for running a separate app called Greyball on certain individuals' phones. Greyball was a shadow app that Uber had developed, with ghost cars and no chance of real rides being taken by these users. Uber installed this version of the app onto the phones of the local law enforcement, the transport authorities and other users who posed a threat to the company – they had no way of knowing what Uber was doing and how it was operating in their towns and cities (Isaac, 2017). They were trying to grow without the authorities being aware, until it was too late for them to do anything about it.

Uber then nearly came undone in 2017 as Kalanick himself faced a crisis of confidence; having been running the employees into the ground, presiding over a sexist culture and with shareholders revolting, he resigned from the role of chief executive officer in June 2017 (BBC News, 2017).

So, Uber is by no means the perfect culture – it absolutely is not the 'poster child', but when we look at the small part of focusing on the need to carve out a market share and drive to profits in a short space of time, the constraints of a start-up certainly acted as a catalyst for its innovation and creativity.

Challenge the status quo

The final example I want to share with you is that of Dick Fosbury. Fosbury is perhaps one of the most influential athletes in modern history and holds a gold medal in the high jump from the 1968 Mexico City Olympic Games (Durso, 1968). He is well known in athletic circles, and indeed outside of them, thanks primarily to his innovation in jumping technique, which is now known as the 'Fosbury Flop'.

The Olympic High Jump changed for ever on 20 October 1968 in Mexico City. The Games were proceeding as normal until 21-year-old Dick Fosbury from Portland took to the field. Fosbury was a civil engineering student from Oregon State University and his physique was unusual compared to the other competitors. Indeed, Fosbury was tall at 6 foot 4 inches, but he had a gangly body and he didn't help his appearance by choosing well-fitting athletic wear; instead he chose mis-matched running shoes to compete in, one being predominantly blue, the other predominantly white.

The high jump was one of the founding competitions of the modern Olympic Games and at the first Games in Athens in 1896 Ellery Clark of the United States took the gold medal with an Olympic record high jump of 1.81 metres (Olympics, 2021). This was a standing jump directly from the floor just slightly behind the horizontal bar that is used to measure the jumps, with the winner being the person who could jump the highest without hitting and dislodging the bar.

The method of jumping over the horizontal bar changed somewhat over the years, but in a very incremental manner. A scissor kick was the first evolution, with competitors running up to the bar and jumping it one leg first. The straddle came next and then the 'Western Roll'. Each time the changes helped competitors raise the bar and jump higher than before. Competitors always took off from their front foot and span round whilst in flight in order kick their trailing leg over the bar first.

Dick Fosbury was inspired by Valery Brumel, a Soviet high jumper who took Silver at the 1960 Rome Olympic Games, and then Gold at the 1964 Tokyo Olympic Games. Fosbury however, wasn't a prolific jumper. *His problem was that his gangly body and unusual frame* wouldn't let him jump to the heights needed to come close to competing at the highest levels of the sport.

His body was the constraint, and he needed a solution – there was no other option. So, he set about taking his engineering knowledge and matched it with what his body was doing as he practised his jumps. Fosbury applied his knowledge and learnt that when he jumped, he was able to keep his centre of gravity below the bar as long as his back was arched perfectly and he led the jump with his front foot, despite the fact his body was jumping over the bar. This was *a technical solution to his constraint.*

In addition to this technical advantage, he also sought a mental advantage. He practised the jumps in his head over and over before the competition and got into a peak mental state, often engaging with the crowd in order to give himself an extra boost and shot of adrenaline just before the jump. These two innovations propelled him to the gold medal, despite everyone writing him off before and during the event.

Sadly, Fosbury never participated in another Olympic Games – he didn't want to; his somewhat introverted personality led him to focus on other things. He had set a new Olympic Record with a jump of 2 meters and 24 centimetres. However, since then, his jump has been copied, replicated and used time and time again, with a new Olympic Record height of 2.39 metres being set with the Fosbury Flop methodology (O'Neill, 2021a). In the final of the 2021 Olympics, Mutaz Essa Barshim and Gianmarco Tamberi ended up sharing the gold medal with jumps of 2.37 metres, agonizingly close to the Olympic Record, both using, you guessed it, the Fosbury Flop (*Guardian* staff and agencies, 2021).

One man's constraint, because of his unusual body shape, ushered in a huge change to an Olympic sport, and the innovation Dick Fosbury designed and shared with the world left a lasting impact on the Games.

Necessity is the mother of invention

So, in closing this chapter, we have seen that it really doesn't matter how much cash you have in the bank, how many people you have, and how many machines or taxis you have – you can still be caught if your culture isn't focused.

You may be a start-up and have very little cash, you may have no choice but to bootstrap your way to success and that is your constraint. You may be limited in labour supply, you may be kept out of a market due to regulations, you may just have an unusually shaped body – all of which means you have to battle these constraints and challenges in order to survive.

Alternatively, you could have all the cash in the world and, seemingly, all the time in the world. But, like we saw with IAG, Bayer and MasterCard, you may decide to create artificial constraints because you know that creativity can thrive in those environments.

As Plato said, 'Necessity is the mother of invention' (to which you can add innovation). When you create, or have, conditions where you have no choice but to move fast, manage change, and outpace your competitors you will surely win versus those who are slow, bureaucratic and unwilling to change.

QUESTIONS FOR REFLECTION

- How do you approach your research and development efforts currently?
- What constraints and challenges could you add immediately to your efforts?
- What topic or business challenge could you run a 48-hour 'innovation express' on?
- Is there anything special or unusual about your company that could be used as a constraint?

In the next chapter we are going to explore our next principle used to create a culture of innovation. We will specifically cover the psychology of individuals and companies, and see how having a 'growth mindset' can play to your advantage when it comes to innovation.

04

Have a growth mindset

In the beginner's mind there are many possibilities, in the expert's mind there are few.

SHUNRYŪ SUZUKI, ZEN BUDDHIST

In this chapter we are going to see one of the most important cultural ingredients for innovation, that of having a growth mindset. And importantly we will learn how to build this kind of culture within companies, specifically by being able to implement high levels of psychological safety.

Psychological safety, first attributed to Amy Edmondson in 1999, *is the belief that you won't be punished or ridiculed for speaking up and sharing ideas and/or feedback* (Edmondson, 1999). It has been shown by multiple studies to be not only a prerequisite for innovation but also an ingredient for the highest-performing teams across industries (Clark, 2020; Hamel and Zanini, 2020; Coyle, 2019).

In return for creating this kind of culture inside companies, the companies are rewarded with innovation, and the employees are rewarded with learning, development and growth. In these environments people work together in order to have the best possible outcomes, and not to gain an advantage over each other or look the best. The interest of individuals is always aligned to the interest of the team or company.

Let us start by learning or reviewing what a growth mindset exactly is.

A growth mindset vs a fixed mindset

These two terms have been popularized by Carol Dweck in her wonderful book *Mindset: The new psychology of success* (2007). If I was forced to make just one book recommendation to anyone, no matter the circumstances, it would almost always be this book. It is a marvellous piece of in-depth research on psychology and Carol Dweck, who is a Professor at Stanford, identifies that people, as well as companies, usually have one of two main types of mindset.

One is the *growth mindset*. This is a mindset where *people believe their success is affected by the time and effort they put into something*. They also *embrace changes, challenges, obstacles* that are put in their way and they learn from and *seek out criticism and feedback* and are *inspired by the success of others*. There is always plenty to go around in a growth mindset perspective: it is a *question of 'and' rather than 'or'*. People who display this mindset believe that they *can get better* and improve at something if they dedicate their time, effort, and energy to it. They believe that they *can improve their flaws* if they practise and persevere. They also believe, perhaps most crucially, that it's *the process rather than the outcome which is the juice*, and the part to be proud of, as the process is where they learn and grow.

The reverse mindset, as Dweck suggests, is a *fixed mindset*. People who have a fixed mindset are most likely to *see their skills as fixed and unchangeable* – their talent or ability for something is innate and they cannot improve. Individuals with this mindset may *avoid challenging situations and difficult environments, and they also give up easily, blame others and ignore feedback*.

In summary, people with a *growth mindset are learners*, always evolving and truly interested in development. Those with a *fixed mindset are focused on natural abilities* and staying still, without taking risk.

Companies as well as people can have cultures of growth or cultures of fixed mindsets. The great news is that a growth mindset absolutely can be taught, and it can be made a reality in any company.

Psychological safety

In my opinion, having studied companies around the world to see what makes them tick, I would suggest that the key component in order to have a growth mindset within your company is psychological safety.

As we know, psychological safety is the belief that you won't be punished or ridiculed for speaking up and sharing ideas or feedback. You can see how this would be important for an individual or a company which wants to grow, learn, evolve and innovate.

My findings from studying innovative companies around the world are reinforced in Carol Dweck's book where she states that *'psychological safety is the number one prerequisite for innovation to occur'*.

Why is psychological safety important?

When you have psychological safety, companies begin to tick. They work like a well-oiled machine and they really start to feel like safe spaces where everyone can contribute equally, without one voice having a more powerful share of the conversation than another, and, because of this, ideas surface easily and change happens. Improvements happen. Innovation happens.

People want to work in an environment that is safe, and they enjoy coming to the office or the factory floor. Everyone participates and people take the chance to learn from their mistakes. As people talk with one another, mistakes are in fact celebrated, and the learning is shared around the company, ensuring the same mistakes are not made again. This gives everyone a spring in their step, and they *have permission to try things*, to go big and go bold. As they bounce ideas off each other and talk things through, openly sharing their feedback and thoughts, the ideas get stronger and with each iteration they are more likely to succeed.

In these kinds of environments, with people enjoying their work, they stay longer (less turnover) (Herway, 2017) and satisfaction is higher (more engagement) (McKinsey & Company, 2021). With people happy and engaged, it cannot fail to translate into the customer interactions and product or service offering. The whole company is stronger.

However, in an environment where mistakes are jumped upon, people live in fear every day that their next mistake, no matter how small, will be ridiculed and there will be a threat to their career prospects. People spend their time watching their backs, dotting the i's and crossing the t's. Instead of taking risks, they become unwilling to rock the boat, and unhappy too. Their ideas are internalized and kept to themselves – there is no conversation in meetings, only dictatorial messages from the top down. People shut down and they lose trust in their teammates and managers, they cannot learn new things, and in order to gain a promotion are all too quick to criticize others and tout their own strengths.

The two types of environments are chalk and cheese, and I am sure that at some point in your career you have experienced both, either on a company-wide scale or a team-level scale.

When you have psychological safety	When you lack psychological safety
• You are willing to take risks and fail.	• Mistakes are ridiculed and laughed at.
• When you make mistakes you use them as an opportunity to learn.	• You stop taking risks, as you are unwilling to rock the boat.
• You share your learning with your colleagues and the company.	• Risk taking is not rewarded.
• Participation is encouraged throughout the working day (debates, conference calls, emails, meetings, town halls, etc).	• Ideas are kept to yourself. • You promote your strengths. • You live in a constant state of fear that one misstep will end your career.
• No matter the level of seniority, everyone contributes.	• You are willing to blame colleagues, and pass the buck.
• There is a high level of authority and ownership taken by individuals.	• There is no speaking up, and instead people nod their heads in meetings.
• You have full confidence and trust in your teammates and managers.	• The most senior voice usually wins, and certainly has the final say on matters.
• There is a commitment to and execution of speaking up, and sharing the truth.	
• Ideas are strengthened by honest and open conversations.	
• You work to make the company or team better, and your focus is on the whole, not yourself.	
• You feel a culture of innovation, learning and collaboration and are happy coming to work.	

Building cultures with psychological safety:
New Amsterdam Hospital

As you know, I am a keen watcher of Netflix. One show (not a Netflix original) that captured my attention during the Covid-19 lockdowns in 2020 was called *New Amsterdam*. This is a TV series about Max Goodwin, who takes up the role as medical director or boss of New Amsterdam Hospital.

The series is based upon the book *Twelve Patients*, which was written by Eric Manheimer, and gave an insight into his thirteen years running Bellevue Hospital in the United States (Manheimer, 2013). As such, much of what is captured in the show is based upon true stories.

Max Goodwin is an up-and-coming doctor without experience of running a major hospital, let alone a hospital that is creaking at the seams due to a lack of funding, excess patient numbers and a huge amount of internal policy and bureaucracy. However, he is an extremely good people-person and, as we later come to learn, a wonderful builder of culture.

The tone is set in the first episode of the series as the new boss begins by asking all the staff to meet him in the atrium for a meeting. He stands at the front of the atrium and tells a story about himself and his sister being born at New Amsterdam Hospital. He goes on to explain that his sister then died in the same hospital aged just eight years old, due to an entirely preventable hospital-acquired infection. He then says that it is a dream come true to work in this hospital as he will have the chance to save someone else's sister, and he smiles.

He then asks the question, 'How can I help?' No one replies. He states that it's not a trick question and he really wants to hear answers. 'How can I help?' he repeats, but still no one answers. So he makes his first bold move by firing all of the cardiac department, as he says that they prioritize billing (sending invoices) above helping patients. The room is shocked, and he asks once again, 'How can I help?' and a lone voice calls out that they want to remove the waiting room for the emergency department and move patients directly into the department without a wait. The request is approved. Then another colleague asks for healthy food to be served in the hospital, and the request is approved.

Max closes the speech, to a now completely stunned audience, by saying that he is willing to get into some trouble to do the right thing and would like to hear more answers to the question of 'How can I help?' moving forwards.

So, what has happened here? Well, someone has clearly come to change a culture, in order to transform a hospital that is not doing so well:

- Max immediately *removed all ambiguity* around the purpose of the hospital, in that it is there to help patients and not to focus on the billing and sending of invoices. As a public hospital it is indeed vital everyone is treated, treated well, and treated equally, not based upon their level of insurance cover.

- Max also has a very *courageous conversation*; he talks about the death of his sister as a child – quite an open and honest thing to mention given you are meeting a whole group of people for the very first time.

- He also *doesn't rush to give advice* when the request to remove the waiting room is made. He follows up by asking 'Where do you want to move it to?' which is a display of empowerment. The response is that the individual in question wants to remove it fully, and this is supported by Max, who says, 'Let us try it then.'

- He closes by asking people to keep escalating concerns and improvements, which is a wonderful way of *reiterating that the door is always open* for these discussions. The tone is set.

Do these points resonate with you? Do you think this is a place where you could work in? Does it look like Max is trying to build a culture where psychological safety is a bedrock?

Hospitals are one of the places where having a great culture of psychological safety is critical. After all, someone not speaking up when they see something wrong, or notice a new piece of information, could be the difference between life or death.

Some practical tips

In order to build psychological safety within your company or team there are a number of really practical things you can do. I share just a few of them below for inspiration, and hope that the subsequent case studies and examples will give you plenty more inspiration to draw from as you go about building a place of work that has a growth mindset fully embedded within it.

TEN TIPS TO BUILD PSYCHOLOGICAL SAFETY

1 Hold, and celebrate, courageous conversations.
   By having courageous conversations, and sharing them in internal communications and messaging, you start to build a culture of openness.

2 Remove ambiguity, mismatches and threats.
   Being explicit and clear in expectations, people will no longer feel that there are shadow boundaries in the workplace, and unwritten rules to follow.

3 Be empathetic and curious.
   By fostering an environment where you make it safe to listen, learn and care about opinions and different views, you build a place that learns.

4 Don't rush to give advice.
   Giving people a chance to solve problems or come to their own conclusions, you are not only empowering them but giving a chance for their innovations to bubble to the surface

5 Clarify roles and responsibilities.
   Similar to removing ambiguity, when people know what they are responsible for they tend to protect, guard and deliver – be clear, and the result will be an environment where people are proud, want to succeed, and will seek out the help and support of their colleagues to do so.

6 Ensure transparency.
   By hiding nothing, you reinforce that everyone is on the same team and you will find that barriers and silos between teams or divisions begin to break, and collaboration increases.

7 Tackle hierarchy.
   Hierarchy often dominates companies, and especially discussions. Ensure that everyone is listened to and avoid 'groupthink'.

8 Ensure appropriate third-party resources, i.e. employee assistance programmes, whistleblowing channels.
   By having these essential channels, you are indicating to the company that it is acceptable to raise issues in an anonymous way and they will be dealt with fairly by a third party.

9 Carry out surveys.
   Give employees a voice, an opportunity to raise their concerns and share their feedback with managers and leaders, and truly listen to and act on that feedback. When actions are visible, the change accelerates.

> **10** Learn from failures, and make them visible.
> *Everyone makes mistakes; successful people and companies learn from them. Don't hide them and risk repeating them. Share mistakes and learning across your company.*

These practical tips, if consistently worked on, will start to change your culture.

When you are next holding a meeting with many attendees, please give a thought to how you can encourage the conversations and avoid hierarchy dominating the discussion. Simple things such as how you arrange the room make a big difference: if you can choose a table, round is always best as everyone is equidistant from the middle. If you have a rectangle table, try to avoid that the most senior person or chairperson sits in the middle with trusted lieutenants either side, as it makes it very difficult for those on the edges to speak up with safety because the hierarchy is visible. And, if you consider it useful, try my favourite tip, which is to invite the most (or one of the most) junior colleagues to give their views and opinions first, rather than the chairperson talking first, anchoring the discussion, and having everyone else nod along, which is always a sign of groupthink and won't get us the culture of innovation we aspire to. Remember, creativity isn't beholden to job title or hierarchy.

I want to focus in further detail on a few of these topics next.

Our school culture

The school system is somewhat curious. We are conditioned throughout our formative years to think that failure is a bad thing. The most important thing is to be correct and score high grades in our papers and tests. If we fail an exam as a child, the most common thing that occurs is to be branded a failure, and often our confidence is knocked. Perhaps in following exams we will re-double our efforts, work harder and learn better than our prior attempt, or, feeling downhearted and with our confidence on the floor we may conform to type and think, 'This is hard, I can't do it'.

Of course, there are some teachers bucking this trend and step-by-step the curriculum is changing and we are valuing skills such as effort rather than exam results. But we have a long way to go.

This system is curious given that when you graduate and leave school, becoming an adult you continue to make mistakes and adults tend to call those mistakes learning, or opportunities to learn.

So, why, in some cultures do we continue to act like we are in school? Imagine this scenario: you are in a meeting and Sam comes in to make a presentation. You have seen Sam work really hard on the presentation, the PowerPoint looks fantastic. There is a new product development opportunity in the presentation that everyone is sure to love. Suddenly, someone notices a mistake in the numbers. But they keep it to themselves. A few people have noticed, though, and everyone smiles throughout the presentation. Sam ends the pitch and the room is lukewarm, neither in favour nor against the new product: nothing is decided. And then, in the corridors after the presentation, people are talking about the mistake in the numbers, questioning Sam's credibility and the new product innovation's soundness.

I am absolutely certain you have been in this type of situation before. Sam is unaware as to why a great innovation hasn't been approved, and, even worse, is unsure of the next steps to take – to keep pushing, or to not rock the boat and stay quiet.

In this scenario, Sam hasn't been giving the opportunity to learn from the mistake in the numbers, and the company as a whole is worse off for it. There was a need to be candid; Sam needed to know the numbers were amiss, the company needed to be able to fairly evaluate the new product. Would it not have been better for all parties if the mistake had been pointed out and there was a chance to put things right? This is difficult to do, of course. However, we need to be able to have this type of brutal or radical discussion when we spot mistakes, or find opportunities to improve upon things. So, we have to learn how to give and receive feedback. Otherwise, these kinds of corridor conversations will continue to harm companies.

Giving and receiving feedback

To me, good feedback is feedback that helps us to understand a situation. The context for the feedback is very clearly on the action or task that the feedback relates to, and then offers support and guidance in what to adapt or change in order to have a better result in the future. This is by far the most difficult cultural change for individuals and companies that is considered in this book, as people simply don't like feedback.

It is not that we don't like feedback generally, because actually most people would like to receive feedback to help them – who doesn't want to know that they have a small mistake in their numbers, or that if they change the colour of ink from black to blue sales will increase by a factor of ten? The trouble is that we have been conditioned with bad feedback, poor-quality feedback, and feedback that doesn't help us to change our behaviours, and thus we consider feedback dangerous, evil and potentially harmful – which in the majority of cases it is.

So, we have to do it right. And doing it right is made possible by two elements: first having a *clear and actionable structure*, and second having *the right environment*, the right cultural climate. These two elements continually appear in leading research from Heen and Stone (2014), the Corporate Leadership Council (2002), and the wonderful experts Bailey and Black, from Mind Gym (2014) – amongst others.

1   A clear and actionable structure:

- Descriptive and evidence based: feedback has to be very clear, ultra-specific and use real examples of situations or data points to justify it.
- Delivered with good intent: feedback has to come from a place of genuine care about the other person, not delivered with a vendetta.
- Future focused: feedback must be actionable in the future, and propose specific, real scenarios or behaviours to change.
- Not only focused on the negative: feedback also has to be focused on strengths of individuals, to help them go from good to great, rather than only focused on mistakes.

2   The cultural climate:

- Fully embed in the culture: meaning that it is normal to give and seek feedback day to day.
- Timely and frequent: feedback must be given regularly and as close to the event that was observed as possible.
- Multidirectional: feedback has to flow in all directions, up, down and sideways – with the same levels of rigour and candour.
- Multichannel: feedback should be given in real time in face-to-face conversations, and it should also be done more formally in writing – there has to be a blend of approaches and tools used.

A clear and actionable structure

Turning our attention to the structure, it is important to use a feedback model to help shape feedback. The one I have found to be most effective is the STARS model. This model is easy to remember, which makes it easy to use, and incorporates all of the key structural elements within it so it should help with delivering or receiving good-quality feedback. I urge you to give it a try:

Situation: Explain the context for giving the feedback.

Task: Share the specific task the feedback relates to.

Action: Describe something the person did, using the real example or data points.

Result: Explain the impact of the action taken.

Support: Share what could be done differently in the future and the likely outcomes.

So, for example, following the model, great feedback could look something like this:

Situation: I would like to discuss the meeting about the new product earlier today.

Task: Specifically the presentation you gave.

Action: You had a great story to tell, but were so enthusiastic you didn't stop for breath and went through it really quickly.

Result: So, people in the room didn't have a chance to raise any questions or doubts.

Support: If you slow down the pace in future presentations, people may be more willing to speak up and interact with you. If you would like, we can practise together.

How would you feel if you received that feedback? I don't think you would be too upset, would you? Probably you would be quite positive and thankful for such clear and actionable feedback.

The cultural climate

When we think about the cultural climate, tools of course make up a large part of the recommendations – but they are not the core. You can have great feedback tools and apps (and there are a vast number of vendors out there who would bite your hand off to sell you their solution) and still not have a culture of feedback – tools only get you so far.

The key is the culture around the use of the tools. In order to make feedback embedded and normal in the day to day, it is important – as well as learning how to give and receive great feedback – that the company is projecting the right messages of support.

First, set out your *reason why feedback is important*. Feedback should be a way to show you care about people, a way to help people grow and thrive, a way to support others in their journey, and help the company be the best it can be. In order to have this kind of culture it is important that you have a very clear narrative about feedback in the company, you set your reason why feedback is important. Any of the reasons just mentioned are strong enough and compelling enough to build messaging around – choose one or two that engage your people with the 'why'.

Second, ensure you *have the capability within the company*. That means everyone is trained in giving effective feedback and receiving feedback. There has to be an awareness that this process is not easy; it makes people feel uncomfortable and tricky conversations and harsh reactions may be experienced. Going through these uncomfortable moments time and time again will slowly make them feel like second nature, but a strong dose of training will be needed up front.

And third, one of the best ways to really change the culture is by *using role models* when it comes to feedback. Seek out role models and highlight them to the rest of the company, use them to spread and socialize the new rules of engagement. If they share their stories of success at town halls, meetings or by leading training sessions on feedback, the belief will soon spread that feedback is useful and helps people within the company.

Learning from your mistakes

The good news is we are now avoiding corridor conversations and everyone is giving and receiving feedback in a wonderful way – thousands of pieces of feedback are flying around on a regular basis. What do we do with this feedback? How do we now make sure that people act upon the feedback, and, importantly when people make mistakes, learn from them?

Successful people, and *successful companies don't hide from their mistakes*. My favourite example of this is Ben and Jerry's – the ice cream company owned by the corporate giant Unilever. This is a company that innovates and tries new things relentlessly, always looking for product innovation.

Most of their time is spent innovating the flavours of ice cream that customers would like and pay for. They launch a number of flavours each year, but they don't always get it right. Whether it is Marshmallow Sky, Whiskey Biz, Butter Pecan, Phish Food, or plain Chocolate they probably have a flavour for your taste buds.

However, they have built a growth culture by using, in part, a very visible symbol that it is acceptable to make mistakes. In Vermont, you will find a patch of land that looks like a colourful graveyard, and that colourful grave-yard is none other than Ben and Jerry's 'Flavor Graveyard'. It is a graveyard full of headstones, for each of the failures in flavours they have had – a very real, visible, representation and sign that they make mistakes and are not perfect or correct all of the time. This graveyard, in jest, shows that they don't hide their mistakes, they learn from them and move on. It shows a level of vulnerability and openness to their employees that says it is safe to fail here – that is the only pathway to success (Ben & Jerry's, 2021).

RULES FOR LEARNING FROM MISTAKES

1 Don't hide from mistakes.
Everyone makes them; the critical difference between success and failure is if we learn from them, and to do that we have to embrace them.

2 Don't feel bad about them.
Don't give yourself a hard time for making mistakes; this is an opportunity to learn and develop.

3 Look to identify the root cause.
In order to not repeat a mistake, it is very important to understand and take action at the root of the cause. Don't be too fast to solve a mistake without diving into it deeply to make sure it won't happen again.

4 Observe patterns.
Identify any patterns in your mistake making – it may highlight a larger theme for improvement, either in your own skills or the company's operations.

5 Know that mistakes are necessary.
Mistakes are a completely natural process of evolution: iteration often leads to improvement.

We have established that a growth mindset is a good thing to have; it helps us grow, develop and innovate. We also know that this type of mindset can only flourish if we have a large dose of psychological safety within our company, and this is a very hard thing to change culturally because we have grown accustomed to bad-quality feedback and prefer, much of the time, to not rock the boat and cause tensions. We also know that giving feedback that is useful is difficult and when we receive it we have to learn from it.

There are a few companies that practise giving and receiving feedback with candour and we will now take a look at some of them.

When it goes right: SpaceX

First up is SpaceX. We touched upon this company in the previous chapter. As the founder, Elon Musk, desires to make humans a multi-planetary species, SpaceX is charged with a very important role.

As you will recall, their first rocket launch, the *Falcon 1*, was attempted only three years and ten months after the founding of the company. They first reached space only a year later, just four years and ten months after the launch of the company, and they made orbit in six years and four months. As of 2021 they are launching *Falcon 9* rockets into space, which have released the most satellites (143 of them) into space in a single mission (Harwood, 2021). They continue to break records and send private individuals into orbit, making it more likely than ever before that the dream of Elon Musk to get to Mars will one day become a reality.

In order to make this dream come true, SpaceX are developing a new type of rocket called the Starship rocket. And this rocket is the backdrop to one of the best displays of psychological safety and willingness to learn from mistakes that I have ever seen.

It was 2 February 2021, and I was tuned into the live broadcast on SpaceX's website which was about to show a new test flight of the Starship rocket, the SN9.

The previous test flight, with the SN8, in December 2020, had seen the rocket fly up into the sky, but explode upon landing – and whilst SpaceX doesn't share the costs of the rocket, theorists online put the price of the rocket's manufacture anywhere from $20 million to $45 million. Either way, an extremely costly piece of kit.

The SN9 had been designed to fly as high as 10 kilometres (6.2 miles), and then return to land at the Boca Chica facility in South Texas. The launch went smoothly, and the rocket flying high in the sky was a thing of beauty – as it gleamed in the sun it was easy to see the day that this design would take cargo and passengers all the way to Mars. Everything proceeded smoothly, it reached its target height and began to re-enter Earth's atmosphere.

However, the rocket was not slowing itself down enough, or returning in a vertical position – and thus, around six and a half minutes after the launch, the rocket hit the ground and exploded, just like the SN8. Another multi-million-dollar mistake had occurred.

However, the Principle Integration Engineer at SpaceX, John Insprucker, was heard on the live video stream saying, '*We had, again, another great flight up… we have just got to work on that landing a little bit.*' Not comments you would have perhaps expected from the one of the people ultimately responsible for the explosion of a piece of high technology worth millions. John proceeded to say, 'As a reminder, this is a test flight, the second time we have launched Starship in this configuration, and we have got a lot of good data' (Sheetz, 2021).

The team at Boca Chica then set to work examining the root cause, and the flight of SN10 in March 2021 saw the rocket land back at the base, more successful than the last, though the landing was a bit bumpy and damage sustained caused it to later explode. SN11 was unsuccessful as well. SpaceX then jumped to version 15 and managed to land SN15 in May 2021 – it was a sight to behold (Chang and Roston, 2021).

This is a great example of a company that continues to iterate and innovate, pushing the boundaries, and has a high tolerance for failure – as long as failure is learnt from. They know that you can design things in a linear way, where you spend years engineering and testing and trying to get everything 100 per cent accurate, or you can go with iterative design and leap from concept to prototype, learning along the way. That is perhaps the greatest clue to why they have achieved so much in so little time.

When it goes wrong: Boeing

When it goes wrong, and companies lack psychological safety and a growth mindset, the results can be stark.

The Boeing Company was founded over 100 years ago in 1916 and has grown in that time to employ a workforce of over 150,000 people around the world. They have innovated as a company for many years and launched the first modern passenger aircraft in 1933, the B-52 bomber in 1952, and highly successful commercial planes such as the 737, which was launched in 1970, have continued to rattle off the production lines. However, since 2018 the company culture has come under the spotlight for the wrong reasons.

On 29 October 2018 a Lion Air flight was about to take off from Jakarta in Indonesia and travel to Pangkal Pinang. A domestic flight that had been taken many times before, but this time the plane crashed into the Java Sea just 13 minutes after take-off, killing all 189 passengers and crew. Then, less than five months later, on 10 March 2019, in a similar event, an Ethiopian Airlines flight from Addis Ababa in Ethiopia to Nairobi in Kenya crashed six minutes after take-off, with all 157 passengers and crew being killed.

Thanks to the in-depth report from the House Committee for Transportation and Infrastructure, published in September 2020, we can see what led to these terrible events that rocked the world of aviation. These two events, utterly disastrous, were strikingly similar. In both cases it transpired that the planes were Boeing 737 MAX models and each crashed because the manoeuvring characteristics augmentation system (MCAS) had activated, pushing the noses of the planes downward, due to faulty data from an angle-of-attack (AOA) sensor, leading to the crashes (United States House Committee on Transportation and Infrastructure, 2020).

Whilst there was a complex series of events that led to these two terrible occurrences and multiple failure points along the line, it is hard, after analysing the House Committee report, to come away with a feeling other than that the company culture had contributed to these events.

Indeed, the report mentions culture sixty times and with 1) a lack of psychological safety, 2) significant financial incentives and 3) employees feeling pressure to produce and working in fear, it is clear the cultural environment was not as it should have been.

Let's take each theme in order, starting with psychological safety. The report found very damning evidence around the culture of speaking up and listening to feedback. Indeed, the investigation found that 'concerns were raised about the MCAS relying on a single AOA sensor' but these concerns 'were not investigated thoroughly enough and in some cases dismissed'. Email exchanges took place where concerns were raised and the issues were marked as 'not a significant concern'. One plant supervisor even waited five weeks for a meeting with the general manager, only to have their concerns dismissed, and then wrote to the CEO and board of directors, without reply, on the same concerns.

The lack of psychological safety is perhaps best demonstrated by the finding that the chief project engineer was unaware when he approved the re-design of the MCAS that it operated from a single AOA sensor, and that in internal tests in simulators pilots had taken over ten seconds to react to un-commanded MCAS activations. The chief project engineer confirmed this in an interview with the House Committee. This indicates that whilst members of the team had data to show there were legitimate and real concerns, they were either suppressed or concealed, perhaps through fear.

The second topic around financial incentives saw Boeing employees actively fight regulations in order to ensure regulators did not mandate the need for flight simulator training of pilots before they could fly the aircraft. The employees knew the plane was similar to previous versions of the 737 plane that came before it, and tried to minimize the appearance of changes because Boeing had massive financial incentive to avoid mandatory pilot simulator training. As just one example, Southwest Airlines had ordered 200 of the 737 MAX and had an option for 191 more, but within the contract was a $1 million penalty Boeing had to pay to Southwest Airlines if simulator training was required.

So, with such sums of money on the line, staff were under pressure to produce and worked in a culture of fear – a key indicator for environments of fixed mindsets. The investigation found that in an internal survey of Boeing employees in 2016 (during the development of the 737 MAX) 39 per cent of employees said they had experienced 'undue pressure' and 29 per cent were 'concerned about consequences if they reported acts of undue pressure'. The House Committee indicated that these were 'disturbing cultural issues' and asked Boeing to 'confront and eradicate conditions that undermine safety'.

This cocktail of financial pressure, fear and lack of leadership that would listen to concerns contributed to catastrophic events that simply must never be repeated. In closing, the House Committee wrote a closing chapter to their report titled 'Time for a culture change' – the culture needed a serious overhaul.

CASE STUDY
Gympass

Gympass is a fitness platform that connects users with over 50,000 partner gyms worldwide for just one single monthly payment. Their goal is to 'make wellbeing universal' and they started on this road in 2012.

Today they count on over 1,000 colleagues globally, and over 4,500 corporate clients that offer the service to their colleagues. And during the global pandemic in June of 2021 the company raised $220 million in Series E fundraising, valuing the business at over $2.2 billion (McCarthy, 2021).

It is headed up by Cesar Carvalho, who co-founded the company and is the Chief Executive Officer. Cesar spent time with me sharing what Gympass do in order to innovate, and explained the six things they have built into their culture to help innovation thrive. Many of the aspects fit this chapter on growth mindset and psychological safety, and thus the case study is positioned here, though there are other elements to draw from, and other chapters will discuss those themes in greater depth.

Gympass's six cultural keys for innovation

1. Clear objectives and ambitious targets

Gympass has built a culture of having '*very clear objectives, a North Star*' and '*ambitious targets*'. Within the company they speak about their North Star metric on a daily basis, and try to optimize all of their efforts around this objective. Cesar explained to me that having everyone in the company know about this goal means there is a strong framework for everyone to push towards. It empowers people to innovate, as no one can block an idea as long as it's with the intention of pushing the company towards their objective, so it acts as an enabler.

2. Ownership mentality

Within Gympass they also value *ownership mentality*. Over 900 current and past employees hold or held equity in the business, and that is deliberate by design. Again, with the idea of knowing their North Star and being enabled to take action, colleagues should act as if they are business owners when they come to work (because they are). This mentality and culture of ownership drives innovation, much like the North Star, as everyone is working in the company's best interest and not their own political agenda.

Despite Gympass being a private company, the equity is tangible and Gympass have gone through seven different liquidity events for staff since their founding (with the most recent being in September 2021).

3. Technology and scalable mindset

The third cultural aspect Gympass has promoted is what Cesar calls 'the technologist/scalable mindset'.

As a small company in their formative years, their teams implemented tactical solutions, and small, temporary fixes for things on a client-by-client basis. That led to great customer service, but ensured the company was missing out on big innovation opportunities. So, they *switched their mindset and they have learnt to plan not for the 4,500 clients they currently have but for the 45,000 clients they will have.*

As a result of 'thinking big' they have empowered everyone to innovate at scale to resolve their most pressing problems.

4. Celebrate failure

At Gympass they are *big on celebrating failure*. The whole company is expected to innovate, and people know it is their job. However, they do have a 'New Venture Area' which is looking at moonshot innovations – the crazy things that no one thinks are possible. There are around 30 colleagues working on these kinds of projects worldwide, and they have a long time horizon.

One of the greatest successes of the New Venture Area has been their self-service platform for small and medium-sized enterprises to sign up to Gympass on. Today, 40 per cent of their new sales come through this channel.

However, perhaps more important for their culture of innovation is to know about their failures, which they celebrate internally. With 50,000 gyms in their network, the New Venture Area tried to launch a marketplace for their partners to buy gym equipment from them at the best possible rates. The negotiation power was supposed to be wonderful, and prices fantastic – but it didn't work. Neither did 'Gympass for kids', and the list continues.

At the end of each failed effort, they celebrate. Of course, it feels bittersweet, because everyone really wanted to make it work, but it's a chance for the team to reflect, to learn, and to recognize that each attempt has taught them something and moves them forward. Cesar knows that psychological safety is critical for innovation to thrive, and failure is not necessarily a bad thing, and certainly not something to punish.

5. Reward

The metrics people are measured on are carefully chosen. Teams like the New Venture Area are measured and rewarded not on revenue targets, or client quotas, but rather on if they have explored the right way, found new ideas to test, etc. Gympass has moved away from 'a formulaic approach to calculate variable compensation for everyone in the company, to a model in which *leaders have more discretion* to rank people and to assign what is the bonus that they make'.

This is key for Cesar, as the company doesn't want people delivering on their objectives through brute force or bad behaviours – whilst pushing the company in the wrong direction. Cesar values people *'doing the right thing'* for the company and its clients, even if it means numeric objectives are not met. He suggests this helps enable people to be more innovative in the way they approach their work, as they are set free from meeting targets that may not lead to long-term benefits.

6. Listening to the ecosystem

And finally, something that Gympass prides itself on 'is creating a company that's talking to customers all the time, then truly listening to them'. The whole team visits gyms and studios and talks to their partners, testing the product and being on the front line. When they sign a new corporate client, they spend time with them, running activation events on site and listening. Just by being with their ecosystem and listening to partners, clients and users they 'have a pipeline of ten years' worth of ideas'. Their work is to prioritize and explore the best or most relevant innovations, and their constant listening means this is constant work.

'When you listen, you are never short of ideas,' says Cesar, who indicated to me that this is perhaps the most important cultural element for innovation to thrive, and he takes immense pride that the whole team is curious and 'knows what is going on in the life of our clients, partners and users'.

Which environment do you want?

It is said that execution environments are designed to be failsafe, but innovation environments are designed to be safe-to-fail.

As Dweck says, 'are you creating a culture of (natural) genius, or a culture of development?' – and which, do you think, has the best chance of success in today's world? I would bet my life that those with a growth mindset and a curiosity to develop and learn each day will win out.

QUESTIONS FOR REFLECTION

- What kind of mindset do you currently have? Does it reveal a growth mindset or a fixed mindset?
- To help foster a growth mindset, what new skill do you commit to learning after reading this book?

- Who are the five people you know who have the best growth mindsets? What traits do they share?
- And who are the five people you know who have the strongest fixed mindsets? What traits do they share?
- How will you foster psychological safety within your company, or team?
- How do you react when someone points out your mistakes? Could you act on the feedback in a better way?
- What will you do in order to get better at giving candid feedback? How can you help your colleagues to develop?
- What will you do to create regular, open, fair debate in your workplace?
- What steps do you commit to taking in order to build a culture of speaking up?

We have just seen how having a growth mindset will encourage innovation, especially when the cultural climate is right and there is an abundance of psychological safety in the workplace. With everyone brimming full of ideas, the next chapter will share some strategies on how best to capture those ideas and filter through them in your quest for innovation. We will explore together how using 'the wisdom of crowds' can lead you to great outcomes, and excellent innovation across any company.

05

Use the wisdom of crowds

None of us is as smart as all of us.

KEN BLANCHARD

We saw in the previous chapter that it is incredibly important to build a culture where people are free to speak up. As well as each person having their own unique voice, and the ability to share ideas, there is a second phenomenon that helps us create value, and that is using the wisdom of crowds.

In this chapter and the next we turn our attention away from the mindset a company needs to foster innovation, and start to consider the impacts partnering with technology can have on the innovation process and the success of companies. In this chapter we are going to see how crowds of people can be smarter than individuals working alone, and how those diverse collaborative efforts, when baked into culture, can lead to innovation in companies.

The wisdom of crowds

The wisdom of crowds, as a concept, really started to come to the fore in 2004 when James Surowiecki published his book *The Wisdom of Crowds.*

In this book, James examined how large groups of people have continually made superior decisions compared to individuals, as long as the crowd follows some basic rules. That is to say, the crowd is diverse, they have independent opinions and are not influenced by one another, they contribute based upon their own knowledge and views, and finally, they aggregate their individual opinions into one collective decision.

The idea of crowds being superior to individuals can be traced as far back as the 4th century BC, to Aristotle's *Politics*. His theory of collective judgement, using food as an example, explained that a feast made by the contributions of many working together would more often than not be heartier than that made by just one cook.

So, pretty compelling evidence that between 384 BC (the birth of Aristotle) and 2004 (the book by James Surowiecki) *the wisdom of crowds effect has been helping people come to better outcomes for a seriously long time* – it isn't a new phenomenon.

Where else does the theory of the wisdom of crowds come into play?

Fairground competitions

One of the best examples of the wisdom of the crowd at play can be seen at fairgrounds.

Often there is a stand for passers-by to guess the number of sweets in a jar, or the weight of a stuffed toy. You pay an entry fee, take a good look at the jar or the toy, and try to run complex mathematical models in your head before writing down your name and guess on a piece of paper. At the end of the day, whoever is closest to the real value wins the sweets or the stuffed toy.

Francis Galton, born 1822, was an English statistician and a legend in the field of science. As well as my favourite piece of research undertaken by him, which was to identify the principles behind the optimal cup of tea, he analysed one such fairground competition in Plymouth, in 1906. At the fairground that day there was a slaughtered ox, and visitors were asked to take turns to guess the weight of the ox. The one whose guess was closest to the ox's actual weight would, at the end of the day, win the ox. Galton took stock of the guesses, and calculated that the median guess was 1,207 pounds. Which was spookily close to the real weight of 1,198 pounds – in fact, the median guess was so close, the error margin was less than 1 per cent (Pearson, 2016).

There are countless examples of this wisdom of the crowd with great levels of success, but before we go on, let me say, unashamedly, that I admit to trying to game the system at fairgrounds myself, by scanning the previous responses on a sheet of paper and making a rough and ready estimation of the average, in order to boost my chances of winning. I don't recall winning yet though… but it has to be just a matter of time.

Collaboration

How can we harness the wisdom of crowds in our companies? What do we need to focus on? Well, in order to have the best chance of the right answer, we need lots of people involved.

Collaboration is now a business necessity, in fact it is one of the superpowers that hiring managers are now looking for, irrespective of the industry, in new candidates.

Work previously may very well have been done successfully within a silo or a business function, but this is no longer the case, in this hyper-connected world. Constant collaboration is a key factor in a company's success, especially when it comes to innovation (World Economic Forum, 2015).

Collaboration is when a group of people come together to work on something jointly in order to produce an outcome. This may be a writer working with a cover designer to produce a book, or a mechanic working with the driver to produce a winning racing car, or the technology department working with the marketing team to ensure the right advertisements are displayed in a shop's point of sale area.

In short, collaboration is group work – or how you work together as a group of people on the same challenge. How well you do this will massively influence the success and outcomes you can achieve in your companies.

Steve Jobs famously summed this up when he was talking about Pixar, the movie studio, and said, 'The important thing is not the idea. It is the people. Our business depends upon collaboration' (*The Pixar Story*, 2007).

WHY COLLABORATION IS IMPORTANT

1 It helps us to problem-solve and innovate.
   Diversity of thought and opinion leads to innovation. As people bring differing perspectives to a challenge or problem, it gets solved more easily.

2 It brings people closer together.
   Silos are one of the main blockers to innovation. By collaborating, people interact with one another and make connections – connections that strengthen over time and help reduce the friction caused by internal boundaries.

3 People learn from one another.
   When people or companies have a growth mindset, they want to learn. When you work across teams or divisions and collaborate on a regular basis you are exposed to new ideas, new ways of doing things and different perspectives that lead you to learn from the experience.

> **4** It boosts morale.
>
> *As you work with people over a sustained period of time, friendships are built and barriers come down. Trust is earned and people become more eager to work in the environment.*
>
> **5** It makes the company a better place to work.
>
> *As people are more eager to work in the environment, and there is increased collaboration, the atmosphere is improved. Employee engagement increases, and it becomes easier to retain existing colleagues and recruit new ones into a great culture.*

Wikipedia

One of the best examples from the modern era that shows what can happen when people get together and work on something jointly to produce an outcome is Wikipedia.

Wikipedia is one of the fifteen most popular websites in the world, according to Alexa Internet, a leading web traffic ranking company (Alexa Internet, 2021). The website continues to garner huge interest from all corners of the world. It is, put simply, group work in the internet age.

Wikipedia recently celebrated its twentieth birthday, having been founded by Jimmy Wales and Larry Sanger in January 2001. It is now available in 323 languages and averages around 15 billion page views each month. That is a heck of a number!

The idea behind Wikipedia is that its pages, comprising of encyclopaedic information on an ever-expanding range of topics and interests, are generated and moderated by the users of the World Wide Web. In practice, as of August 2021, its just under 54 million pages of content are managed and updated by a team of just under 300,000 volunteers across the globe (Wikipedia, 2021).

As Wikipedia expanded from the late 2000s onwards, it had its fair share of criticism aimed at it for reliability and bias in the content, but then, as more users started to contribute – through the wisdom of the crowd – the pages have become much more accurate, the quality of writing has improved, and bias has been reduced. More eyes working together to moderate the content made for a better product.

Collaboration has clearly worked in this case, and it's a good example of product innovation, as humans did indeed have encyclopaedias before the internet came along, if you can recall those heavy books?

Where ideas come from

We already know that if we collaborate with a wide range of people, with diversity of thought, great outcomes can be achieved. One interesting example of this is from World War II.

A statistician, Abraham Wald, was working at a company called the Statistical Research Group when they were asked during the middle of the war effort by the American military to take a look at the fighter planes that had returned from missions and identify where would be the most suitable places to add some extra bullet-proof armour, so that fewer planes were shot down and more would return home safely.

Wald was born in Hungary in 1902 and graduated from the University of Vienna with a doctorate in mathematics, before immigrating to the United States. His contributions, in addition to this piece of work for the military, included the creation of a new formula for the cost of living index. Wald was widely recognized as one of the most brilliant statistical minds before his untimely death at the age of 48 in 1950, in a plane crash in India.

As Wald began his work, the military provided him with a comprehensive view of all of the bullet holes in the planes that had returned from battle. It was clear to see that the area in and around the fuselage had taken a lot of bullet rounds and the military were ready to reinforce this area. Fortunately, they had asked for the outside help and support from the Statistical Research Group, and as a result of this outside perspective, the Group reasoned that the military had provided data on planes that had returned and thus the fact that they had taken bullet rounds in the fuselage area and returned may actually indicate that this was not a particularly troubling place to have taken the shot. However, as the data did not highlight many bullet rounds in the engine space, Wald reasoned that this would be the area best suited to reinforcement. Of course, this was the right answer and the planes were reinforced and subsequently achieved greater success, with more successful missions and more pilots returning home safely (Mangel and Samaniego, 1984).

So, the moral of the story is that the best ideas often come from outside, and instead of asking ourselves where they come from, we perhaps need to ask ourselves where do they not come from and then search there.

Everyone can copy, replicate and conform. If we look for the answers where they are most obvious we are surely missing opportunities to innovate. Ideas should come from your customers, employees, partners, suppliers, competitors and external experts – but how often do you consult these stakeholder groups in your company?

We have to *make an effort to engage with more diverse opinions* than ever in order to take advantage of the phenomenon that is the wisdom of crowds. And there is one new technology that has been helping companies exploit crowds at scale for a few years now: the internet.

Crowdsourcing

As we look to plug our blind spots and think differently by engaging with crowds of different stakeholders, the internet has made this much easier. With 4.66 billion people connected to the internet as of early 2021 (Johnson, 2021) (and the number bound to increase to 8 billion-plus people in the coming months and years as the internet becomes even more democratized and available to all at low costs to entry) there is a crowd at everyone's fingertips, and a very diverse one too (Diamandis, 2018).

Crowdsourcing is defined as the practice of obtaining information or input to a task or project by enlisting the services of a large number of people, either paid or unpaid, typically via the internet.

Crowdsourcing is a fancy solution or word for what people have been doing for a number of years through focus groups, interviews and surveys of customers and the like. However, the advantage now is very much the internet's speed and scale.

A wide range of companies have sprung up over the past few years offering online solutions for your crowdsourcing needs, connecting people with challenges and surfacing the most relevant ideas to the top for a company to take action upon, or, even better, solutions already developed and ready to be implemented.

Internet-based crowdsourcing

You may have heard of companies such as Google, IBM and The LEGO Group undertaking crowdsourcing challenges internally with their employees. Charities and public bodies like the National Health Service in the United Kingdom are also crowdsourcing solutions to help them with some of their most pressing issues.

Asking questions via online platforms, they allow their employees to anonymously respond with their solutions and feedback (the anonymous part is very important as it means ideas win rather than hierarchy and when people add their views to the platform it doesn't make any difference if they are the CEO or an intern). With the responses made public to everyone in the company, other colleagues vote and rate them, comment and reply with their own improvements, enhancements or doubts. Debate is held, all online. And, after a short time, the best solutions surface to the top. This is becoming standard practice in many companies.

However, this type of crowdsourcing is not limited to just employees; many are starting to engage their outside stakeholders (such as their customers, communities and shareholders) to help with their innovation efforts.

There are two major platforms that have caught my eye and that I'd like to bring to your attention. The first is XPRIZE. XPRIZE is a non-profit organization which was founded by Peter Diamandis in 1994, based in the United States. Peter is a multiple business owner, and as well as being founder of the XPRIZE he also co-founded Singularity University, which is a business incubator and education provider with an eye on the future. Teaching courses about innovation and future technologies is one of the main focuses at Singularity University.

So, it comes as little surprise that XPRIZE is also focused on the future. The XPRIZE concept is formed around crowdsourcing solutions to important high-profile problems that the world faces, often providing a prize to the winning solution, or funding for its implementation. The prizes are provided by public figures in most cases. For example, the XPRIZE competition of 2020 saw the XPRIZE team ask for teams to design next-generation face masks in response to the Covid-19 pandemic (XPRIZE, 2020). The competition had a total of $1 million in prize money, and was sponsored by Marc Benioff, the CEO of Salesforce, and Jim Cramer, the host of the TV show Mad Money. They asked 16- to 24-year-olds to come up with 'more comfortable, functional and affordable' masks to fight the coronavirus pandemic.

Just under 1,000 entries were gathered and a team of students from Arizona State University in the United States took home the $500,000 first prize for their design of an anti-fog face mask. Their mask design saw air exhaled from the nose being kept in a separate chamber from the face and mouth, which led to fresher air being breathed in and air flowing away from glasses, which would otherwise become foggy. As a result of their win, the new mask designs were put into production in the United States.

The largest prize so far was offered by Elon Musk in 2021 (XPRIZE, 2021), and is a $100 million prize for those who can remove massive quantities of carbon from the climate. The competition is ongoing, and garnering a lot of interest.

The second platform, called Herox, is an off-the-shelf software platform that lets companies post their own challenges around problems they need to solve, and then anyone in the world is free to post their ideas and solutions in response. People can work as teams or individuals on the platform. Companies like NASA, IBM and The Coca-Cola Company have used the platform with great success.

A very important item to be aware of when thinking about launching a crowdsourcing challenge is that you do need to have a lot of participation. The more the merrier, as research has proven that more successful innovation occurs when companies have higher ideation rates. Companies which foster high ideation rates internally, that is to say, they have more employees participating and more ideas being generated, also generate increased net profits (Minor et al, 2017). However, this is easier said than done. Companies need to welcome ideas from their employees in order to have them freely generate and share their ideas. Fortunately, Pete Thomond, the Chief Executive and founder of Clever Together, shares how to do this in the next case study.

CASE STUDY
Clever Together

Pete Thomond has had a fascinating career thus far. Holding a PhD in Disruptive Innovation from Cranfield University, UK, Pete's work has taken him across the globe, helping companies with their innovation efforts. Pete dedicated his PhD to disruptive innovation and studied it via various lenses, such as the psychology of innovation, the technical management of innovation, and innovation strategy, and then spent time researching and consulting in Australia in the same field. After this stint in academia Pete decided he wanted to have a direct impact on innovation, and moved back to the UK to found his companies, Clever Together and Sport Inspired, which are filled with smart people working on important topics.

The story of Clever Together, and his other venture, Sport Inspired, showcases crowdsourcing as they both use an 'asset-based approach' to innovation (making use of the value the community can bring), with Clever Together focused on creating better solutions, through crowdsourcing, to pressing challenges, and Sport Inspired helping young people live more healthily and be more active.

Pete was kind enough to invest a significant amount of time in this book, and through a series of interviews has shared his approach to innovation. His passion for the topic shone through loud and clear, and what follows are some very useful and practical insights for innovation as a whole, but in particular crowdsourcing – which is the area of expertise at Clever Together. Clever Together is an agency that helps individuals and companies to understand their challenges, and solve them with the help of their crowdsourcing methodology. To date, Clever Together have engaged over 500,000 people in challenges, and that is just with their public sector clients. Their history of supporting innovation obviously traces back to Pete's research days, and since then they have helped their clients to innovate and prosper for over twelve years.

On collaboration

The whole team at Clever Together consider that the *collective intelligence of a group is always more than the intelligence of an individual*, and there is always more knowledge outside of a room, than inside it. Their job is to help their clients seek out that knowledge and put it to good use. As a result of these beliefs, throughout our conversations Pete highlights that, logically, there is *a natural limit to the innovation that a small group of people can have*. So, whenever you set out on a crowdsourcing effort the key is to find a way to harness that collective intelligence and to do that through *active collaboration and with high involvement or open innovation* methodology, i.e. where people are collaborating in a meaningful and frequent manner. Pete explained that academics have proven that innovation and collaboration go hand-in-glove, and when we remove the limits in terms of intelligence levels of small groups or individuals, and expand the net, the results can be overwhelmingly positive. Pete calls this tapping into the '*collective brilliance*' of people.

In addition to innovation arising from crowdsourcing, it should also be noted that these efforts, done well, frequently lead to an improved sense of belonging, camaraderie, sense of pride in the company, etc. So, there are many extra benefits to this type of engagement.

On running a successful crowdsourcing challenge

Running a successful challenge isn't an easy endeavour, and there are plenty of pitfalls as you introduce these challenges in your companies. Tools are most often not the answer to a company's innovation problems, and indeed are often the source of frustration and blame when things go wrong, so it is important to understand the facets of a solid campaign before beginning.

Just as you would expect bad results, and possibly even detrimental results, if you gave a hammer and paint brush to a non-DIY person, the same will happen with crowdsourcing efforts if not well executed. You may find yourself implementing the wrong things if you have asked the wrong question. You may follow the wrong leads if you cannot interrogate the data well, and then you will disenfranchise your stakeholders who joined in with the process.

However, with strong planning and the right culture there are methods to ensure you have the best chance of success. There are four key areas to focus on and consider when embarking upon a crowdsourcing challenge. They are:

1 The mandate

2 Interest generation

3 True insight

4 Actions

Firstly, *the mandate* relates to having a strong and clear commitment from leaders in the company towards the challenge that is about to be launched. Typically, there are three sub-elements within the mandate:

- *Leaders* need to ensure that their teams feel *genuinely connected* to, and *trust* that actions are really going to happen.

- The second element is that there is a truly *meaningful challenge* and conversation, and it is *well defined and clear*.

- The third is that it is a *time-bound* challenge where they *promise* to deliver something as a result of the challenge.

These three elements combined mean that the leader or leaders who are launching an innovation challenge are publicly putting themselves on the line and saying to their workforce, 'Here is our promise to you, we have a challenge that we need your help with, there are impacts to doing nothing, but if we find a good solution the upside is x, and this is our promise to act'. At this initial stage in the challenge, indeed at the start of the considerations, the leaders need to be aware that embarking upon a challenge but not following through may very well be detrimental as people lose confidence, interest and belief in the leaders, and thus the innovation efforts. So, it is important, up front, to be fully committed to time-bound action.

Once you have got the mandate clear, and are committed to action, you can take the well-defined and clearly articulated challenge and begin to embark on *interest generation*. The key here is to craft beautiful communications that encourage the various stakeholder groups to participate. There will be a number of different stakeholders you want to engage with during a challenge, and often the more groups you engage, the better, thanks to the diversity of views they will bring. *Each group needs to be afforded individually tailored and targeted messaging.*

Once you have captured the imagination and interest of the people you want to target, you then need to generate *true insight*. This is the process of crowdsourcing, and often it is a blend of physical and digital actions. You may *launch a digital platform* to capture a wide range of feedback and insight into the challenge, but you may also *need to capture some of this data physically*. You *need to reach people where they are*, not where you want them to be. You owe it to the innovation effort and the challenge to reach your stakeholders, as everyone's voice is just as rich and important as the next. This may mean that you hold meetings in the canteen and ask people to add sticky notes to a whiteboard – many people don't read emails and won't join online efforts, and a *blended method to capture input from lots of people* is critical.

Then, once you have the qualitative information, *the juice is in the analytics*. It is important to have people who can analyse qualitative information: some data will be in digital platforms, other data points will be the sticky notes you collected from the canteen. You have to *drill down into the conversation*, and look for the connecting factors. Thematically analyse the data, look at the themes, look across themes to find insight you didn't expect.

The trick then is to *take the insight back out to the people*, saying, 'Here is what we think we have heard – do you agree or did we miss anything?' At this stage, you socialize the solution ahead of time and validate it. You should be prepared for some resistance, particularly if the solution or change is radical. As the saying goes, 'Turkeys don't vote for Christmas', but 'Innovators have to improve what we do with one hand, whilst create the new with the other' – and when there is this resistance it often means you are onto something.

Finally, once the insight has been validated, and refined if needed, you should go into the *action* phase. The action phase is about *going back to the mandate and honouring the promises you made*. However, here you shouldn't just do and deliver what you set out to do, that is the minimum, *but you should spend a lot of time in talking about what you have done*. It is critical you close the loop well here, and *people need to see and feel your actions*. This is your moment to reinforce the behaviour of innovation that you have just had across the company, and boost the sense of collective pride and involvement (which boosts retention and engagement).

On nervousness

Of course, it is natural that people become nervous in the lead-up to a crowdsourcing challenge, and during it. There are predominantly two motivations behind this nervousness:

- leadership nervousness
- general change nervousness

If we *consider leaders, many do tend to get nervous*. They often become *worried about the optics of the challenge, and how they will be seen*. However, to support those leaders, it is important to position the challenge as something positive for the company, the greater good, and be clear that this is not an attack on their work or position – the purpose is improvement. In the end, if they are nervous it is usually because people already know some of the less than positive optics and talk about these behind closed doors. So, the choice leaders have at this stage is to *either embrace the topic and use it as a chance to improve, or ignore it – in which case it will simply persist*. When you know you have these two choices, and the latter means you will continue to be the topic of conversation, it is often easier to accept it, join the conversation and get involved. The risk of joining the conversation is definitely lower than the risk of ignoring it.

In terms of the *general change nervousness*, it is also true that people become nervous for similar reasons to the leaders and revert to thinking '*This is my job, and this is how I do it – so I don't want to change or have people suggest improvements.*' In this case, Clever Together have found that around 80 per cent of what is crowdsourced during a challenge was already known to the experts working on those topics, and the crowdsourcing is useful as it gives people the momentum or push to make a change. If you have *the power of a crowd behind you, it's a social movement*. It is no longer one person pushing for a change, but a crowd: so it is safer. When lots of people are agreeing or proposing an approach or course of action, it's much more difficult to keep banging your own drum in the opposite direction (either refusing an innovation or slowing it down – which can often be the case in a more hierarchical approach to decision making and innovation). The *sense of social movement through crowdsourcing helps overcome nervousness*.

On encouraging participation

Nervousness is just one common challenge that you will face during your challenge. You may also face *participation challenges* – and you need to address this upfront, before you launch a challenge.

There are two things you can do to promote participation. The first is that leaders need to *be explicit* to their stakeholders when they share the challenge, and really impress upon them that everyone has a responsibility to speak up and share their views as *innovation is everyone's responsibility*. No longer is innovation the job of a small group of people in a laboratory. The companies that are doing this best are the ones that make this responsibility explicit to their people.

The second thing to promote participation is to ensure there is *psychological safety*. As we saw in the chapter which covered having a growth mindset, there are a number of techniques that you can deploy to encourage and foster psychological safety across a company. Those hints and techniques aligned closely with Pete's recommendations.

Without a clear dose of responsibilities and expectation, as well as psychological safety, you may find less than optimal levels of engagement, or, even worse, engagement that fails to share the root cause of problems and masks the truth.

On the word 'innovation'

One closing topic we discussed was related to the word 'innovation', and specifically the negative or 'scary' connotations it can have with certain groups of people. Pete has a very academic background, and of course has a very academic definition of innovation. However, most people hear the word and think one of two things. They think there will be *bright, shiny, new stuff*. Or, they will think that they are about to be *forced, grudgingly, into some sort of change*.

If it is the case that the word causes hairs to rise in your company, Pete suggests *using the language 'adaptive, creative and positive' to have people often come on board just that little more*. Pete's wording can soften even the hardest people, as an adaptive company is one that is changing, so that they survive in hard times and thrive in the good. They do that by being creative, and because everyone is contributing they are positive places where everyone wants to work – which doesn't sound too bad to me.

Non-internet crowdsourcing

Of course, using the internet or digital mediums to crowdsource isn't the only solution, and below I would like to turn our attention to those who have pioneered different approaches to crowdsourcing that don't utilize the internet.

Crowdsourcing physically within your own four walls

One of the companies that has been pioneering a crowdsourcing approach for a number of years now is Pixar, the creative studio behind our favourite films such as *Toy Story* and *Finding Nemo* to name but a few.

Pixar has had a long and colourful history, with the company being formed after its spin-off from Lucasfilm, the film production company founded by George Lucas of *Star Wars* fame. The computer graphics division within Lucasfilm was bubbling along, with little support from its owner, and even less capital – despite having the aim of bring the world of films into the digital era by using computer-generated imagery in films. In 1986 Ed Catmull and Alvy Ray Smith, two computer scientists, went on to agree a separation of the computer graphics division and turned it into a stand-alone company called Pixar.

As a start-up, Pixar sought funding and settled upon Steve Jobs, who had been removed from his company, Apple, at the time. Jobs became the majority shareholder and funder of the company. Jobs liked the vision that Catmull and Ray Smith shared with him about the opportunities which computers brought to the film industry, and throughout the next ten years the team at Pixar battled financial troubles and a number of technical challenges before hitting upon their first great feature-length film in 1995, that being *Toy Story*, which was directed by John Lasseter, and set the foundations for even greater success.

Toy Story was the first feature-length film using computer-generated imagery and its success exceeded the wildest imaginations of both Pixar and Disney, which was its partner at the time. Steve Jobs had stated that 'if the film makes $75 million we will break even, $100 million we will both make money and at $200 million, a box-office blockbuster, we will make good money' (Afuah, 2014). Well, the film grossed over $350 million in worldwide sales and Pixar had landed on its own two fect (IMDB, 1995).

However, following the release of *Toy Story*, the company didn't have smooth waters to sail in as innovation is rarely easy. Pixar knew that the tricks and visuals that worked on their previous movie wouldn't necessarily work for their next one and they had to continue to innovate and push themselves from within, creating a culture where they became naive once again and challenged every assumption.

One of the methods they have used within Pixar to ensure their movies are the best they can be is a form of crowdsourcing that they call 'The Braintrust'. The idea of this Braintrust came about as a result of reflections from the production of *Toy Story* when five of the key players involved in the film bounced ideas off of one another and solutions clicked.

The Braintrust expanded, and is now a large group of people, from all areas of Pixar, who meet on a regular basis to review and discuss the movies the team is working on. The idea of the Braintrust meeting is that a great number of smart, and passionate, people are put into a room together to give open and honest feedback on how to solve problems and enhance the films Pixar is making. People collaborate with one another to get the best outcome, surface new ideas and solutions and help by supporting the writers or directors when they are lost. The wider group of people helps to bring a different perspective and often suggest new courses of action that have not been thought about before.

Steve Jobs had already noted that 'our business is collaboration' and the director, John Lasseter, was clear that creatively 'Pixar is its people' (*The Pixar Story*, 2007). The Braintrust approach, moulded by these two perspectives, is to this day a ritual that continues and has contributed to more modern-day film success in the form of the films *Soul* and *Luca*. By having the honest, candid and well-intentioned feedback from numerous people early on in the design process, the films have been enhanced as each contribution has added, or 'plussed' to the final output.

In 2006 Disney, which was a partner on Pixar productions, notably *Toy Story*, bought Pixar at a valuation of $7.4 billion (La Monica, 2006). One interesting outcome of the transaction was that Walt Disney Feature Animation had been struggling since the late 1990s and into the early 2000s. The division within Walt Disney Studios wasn't performing well financially, was failing to produce box office hits, and started to downsize its organization, making redundant a number of employees and starting severe cost cutting. The division continued to haemorrhage money and in 2005 the newly appointed CEO of Disney, Bob Iger, started to look at the underlying business. He was later quoted as saying he 'did not (at the time) have a complete sense of just how broken Disney Feature Animation was' (Disney Fandom, 2021).

As Bob set about his work, he approved the purchase of Pixar, and agreed to the two companies being kept separate. In his online Masterclass, Bob explains that when buying a company that is successful you are often buying a company which has a great culture, one that you need to foster and keep apart from your existing business, or risk destroying what makes it valuable and attractive as a purchase in the first place. Clearly, Bob had, in part, bought Pixar because of its great culture that led to success in its film productions (Masterclass, 2019).

With this in mind, the two companies were kept separate, but over time various practices pollinated from one side to the other. Perhaps the biggest cross-pollination occurred when Disney introduced 'Crit Sessions' which were very much aligned to the Braintrust. In these sessions, teams of colleagues from across Walt Disney Animation Studios (as it was and is now known, following a name change in 2007) came together to give candid feedback and help fix parts of scripts that were not flowing, or improve elements of the production. A little later the division of Walt Disney Animation Studios was on fire once again, and *Frozen* was a smash at the box office, thanks in no small part to the crowdsourced solutions of the Crit Sessions.

As well as these sessions seen at Pixar and Disney, Chris Rainey, who hosts the 'HR Leaders' podcast which regularly pulls in 500,000 subscribers, reminded me in a discussion of innovation happening within internal Employee Resource Groups (ERGs) that 'innovation often comes from connection' and, especially in a time where remote work is more dominant, those connections need to be fostered. Chris explained to me that a number of companies had been busy, during the pandemic, launching ERGs, which are groups of colleagues that come together to discuss a specific topic, often around a shared interest or identity. For example, Cargill, the American food manufacturer, has achieved innovation by using their ERGs to help them define how they should enter new markets. Local ERGs on the ground got together and mapped out a way forward, putting aside their day-to-day, hierarchical responsibilities during the process.

Crowdsourcing with your competition

But crowdsourcing need not only occur within your own four walls. Often looking outside of your home comforts is richly rewarded.

The LG Corporation, based in Seoul, South Korea, is one of the world's foremost conglomerates focused on the fields of electronics, telecommunications, technology and energy. It is highly likely you have watched your favourite TV show on an LG-manufactured television, or use an LG mobile phone, or perhaps you have used a washing machine or refrigerator made by LG.

What may surprise you is that in order to exploit the wisdom of crowds in their field of work, LG has taken the approach to partner with rivals, and its competition, in order to continue innovating. LG has seen the power of open innovation platforms and is forging a path to success, together, with its competition. That sounds like teamwork and collaboration in the greatest sense to me, and goes completely against the grain of keeping ideas to one's self in order to safeguard and protect them.

The LG Innovation Council programme was launched in July 2020, and is formed of twelve future technology experts from around the world. They include experts in the fields of artificial intelligence, big data, the cloud, robotics and mobility. Colleagues from Paypal, Amazon, Baidu, and Cisco, amongst others, were invited to be founding members of the Council with the aim to learn from each other and find opportunities for new collaborations.

As the President and Chief Technology Officer of LG Electronics, Park Il-Pyung, remarked at the Consumer Electronics Shows in January of 2021, 'we have to work with others and innovate as a team' (LG, 2021). I imagine that in the space of just a few months, we will be watching LG televisions or using LG washing machines that have benefited from the insight this network of experts has contributed to.

Crowdsourcing with the world

The world is our oyster in this digital, hyper-connected age, and we need not limit our innovation efforts to just our four walls, nor those of our competition.

According to Statista, as of the first quarter in 2021, the Google Play app store hosted 3.48 million apps and the Apple app store hosted 2.22 million apps for our mobile devices (Ceci, 2021). The vast majority of these apps are not Google or Apple produced; in fact the concept of the app store is perhaps the most successful display of open innovation and crowdsourcing in the modern age.

Apple and Google quickly learnt that their core business was not creating swathes of apps for our devices but rather providing a store front for those apps to be sold to, or downloaded by, consumers across the world. They cottoned on to the fact that there are pretty much an unlimited number of solutions that could be designed in the form of apps, and rather than try and create them all themselves, decided to enable an open innovation platform where the best app (and innovations) could be provided to their clients by harnessing the wisdom of the crowd.

However, it is not only the technology giants that are using the power of the crowd across the world. Johnson & Johnson, the pharmaceuticals company based in New Jersey, United States, also help to foster the wisdom of the worldwide crowd through their JLABS programme (JLABS, 2021).

JLABS is one part of the Johnson & Johnson Innovation family of companies. Johnson & Johnson has a wide range of companies operating in the innovation space, from a business development group designed to help later-stage companies, through to a venture capital fund and various innovation centres for early-stage companies. JLABs is the most interesting to me because it is an open innovation ecosystem which offers support to innovators and inventors of new scientific discoveries.

When companies enter JLABS they gain access to a global network of industry connections, special research opportunities, training and mentoring, and a community of likeminded entrepreneurs – as well as no-strings-attached financial assistance. The beauty of this crowdsourcing solution is that Johnson & Johnson have no financial incentive linked to the company. They don't invest in the companies nor do they demand a stake of the equity for participation. It is truly a network for connecting and contacting with others – and as of August 2021 there were 544 companies working within the JLABS network to push the boundaries of the healthcare sector. These companies are taking advantage of the wisdom of the crowd by collaborating with others in Johnson & Johnson office space, and networking using the virtual conferencing facilities Johnson & Johnson have set up to facilitate connectivity between the companies and the experts across the industry. This is an example of a true open network platform, with massive collaboration, which yields results.

Outside of these for-profit enterprises we also see government agencies using forms of crowdsourcing as a conduit to their innovation. The Pentagon's Defence Advanced Research Projects Agency (DARPA) has the responsibility for development of new technology and capabilities in order to ensure the technical superiority of the United States military. DARPA was created in 1958 in response to the Soviet Union launching the Sputnik satellite into space, and has been very successful over the years with its innovation efforts, having played a part in developing satellites, drone technology, the global positioning systems, and most recently helping the innovation to develop the Moderna mRNA vaccine against Covid-19 (by awarding Moderna $25 million back in 2013 to help develop the Messenger RNA technique for delivering medicine) (PR Newswire, 2013). Indeed, DARPA has been so successful that the President of the United States, Joe Biden, in 2021 asked Congress for funding of $6.5 billion in order to set up a DARPA equivalent for health with the ambition to 'end cancer as we know it', and he won't stop there, with plans for a climate change body also in the works (*The Economist*, 2021).

DARPA has been so successful because it focused on the wisdom of the crowd. Rather than take its $3 billion annual budget and spend the money internally on thousands of staff and mountains of equipment to fill vast laboratories, DARPA spends its energy on designing challenges and clearly articulating their problems before collaborating with others, crowdsourcing the best solutions and then funding their development. This means that DARPA is a very fluid organization, one with permeable boundaries: it is always in a state of transition (Dugan and Gabriel, 2013).

DARPA's advantage is that it defines a problem, appoints internal project leaders, and then many companies compete to tender for funding and creation of the solution. This means it has the pick of the companies to choose from, and because DARPA is not afraid to change course during the project, they often focus on short sprints of activity. As such, were they developing a cyber security system, they may partner with a wide range of external contractors and experts throughout the project lifecycle in order to tap into the best and the brightest as they go along, which is a big change compared to many companies who partner with an external partner for the whole duration of the project, expecting them to deliver on everything under the sun.

Working with the best experts, for the most appropriate challenges, or sprints, means great flexibility and more value for money. As their results suggest, this is one kind of crowdsourcing approach to innovation that can have us reaching for the stars.

We is almost always smarter than I

So, with many ways of gaining the wisdom of the crowd, from very basic fairground games and a sheet of paper, through to online digital competitions that exploit the connectivity of the internet, through to the creation of cross-division working groups, cross-company working groups, and even the creation of open innovation platforms, there are many ways to hunt for innovation.

With people working across the world, and talent being dispersed across the planet leveraging the crowd, this is one of your greatest opportunities. We have an abundance of resources at our fingertips, and a market of 4.66 billion people (and growing) to tap into – one which is extremely diverse and available 24/7. The *cognitive surplus that is just sitting, waiting, for their excess capacity to be put to good use* could really drive you on to building your next set of products or services, irrespective of your company size.

When you have a culture of *asking for input*, and *letting the best ideas win* – rather than hierarchy – you are well on your way to innovation. Access to diverse pools of thinking is no longer difficult, the diversity is no longer scarce; the wisdom of the crowd is at our fingertips and crowdsourcing will push us forward, as long as we know the right questions to ask and challenges to pose.

We is almost always smarter than I.

QUESTIONS FOR REFLECTION

- Who or what groups of stakeholders do you currently ask for input from?
- Where are you currently not looking for answers? Are you missing the opportunity to consult with your customers, employees, partners, suppliers, competitors or external experts?
- What challenge(s) could you pose to this wider group of stakeholders?
- Do you have problems that you are very close to and cannot see a way forward on? Could crowdsourcing help you?
- Which method or technique from the chapter will you choose first in order to get more people helping you with the next problem you face?

In the next chapter we are going to explore why it is important that your culture embraces new technologies, and doesn't choose to run away from them – in order to drive innovation. The world is always changing, and much of this change is as a result of new technology (5G, AI, etc) and it needs a very deliberate effort and focus on culture to ensure that you embrace technology, rather than shy away from it. The coming chapter will unpack some examples of where those who have moved in tandem with new technology have succeeded (proactively), and how technology has helped others (reactively) to stay the course during difficult times. We will look at some practical approaches to how you can embrace technology, and build this into your culture, much of which is based upon your willingness to partner with technology.

06

Embrace technology

Technology is the solution to human problems, and we won't run out of work till we run out of problems.

TIM O'REILLY, FOUNDER OF O'REILLY MEDIA

As we saw in the previous chapter, technology offers us some great advantages when it comes to being able to engage large crowds of people to exploit their collective wisdom. However, that isn't all that technology offers us. Technology in the modern age really is a bedrock of innovation, especially as we enter this exponential age where change continues to happen at an ever-increasing speed.

The differences we can see between those who have embraced technology and those who have shied away from it are stark reminders of the importance of spending time getting to grips with technological trends, and doing plenty of research, so that when the time is right you can take full advantage of them.

Culturally, we have to fight against the short-term view, the risk to jobs, the potential redundancy of our existing investments, and the egos we have which tell us that we know better than a computer programme. Our innovation efforts are much more successful when we choose to deliberately partner with technology.

Digital transformation and innovation through technology is inherently a culture change programme, one that arises through a need to adapt the mindset of a company: to help companies recognize that technology is business, and business is technology. Technology is not just a bolt-on to existing structures, it needs to be ingrained deep within the culture to work well – so there is a true partnership.

Web 1.0

The internet changed the world. Designed in the 1970s, with DARPA playing an important role in its development through the provision of grants to various universities and research centres around the world, the internet connected computers together, leading to computer networks full of machines that could talk and interact with one another. Though the general public would only start to become familiar with the internet in the early 1990s, many innovators were busy working on ways to utilize the internet, and the creation of the World Wide Web, electronic mail and social media have since followed.

The World Wide Web was the application which supercharged the world. Invented in 1989 by British inventor Tim Berners-Lee, the World Wide Web allowed computer users to access digital information that was stored online (World Wide Web Foundation, 2021).

The first iteration of the World Wide Web was a 'read only' environment. People would log onto their web browser using dial-up connections that would send sharp noises down the phone line to anyone who dared pick up the receiver, and would search for information and read it. At this stage, there was very little by way of user interaction with web pages and there was even less content generation occurring.

Businesses would tend to use the web as an extension of their brochures or leaflets, uploading static text and images that displayed their company's goods or services, for anyone to read – no longer hampered by the need to send a brochure via the postal service to a customer. Their potential customer base suddenly jumped from being those who lived close to the shop, to anyone who was connected to the web from around the world.

However, the internet, and specifically the World Wide Web, was repeatedly bashed over the head by all and sundry. Some journalists accused the internet of being a 'passing fad' with 'millions were turning their back on the world wide web, frustrated by its limitations' (Chapman, 2000). Not only was there negative media coverage, there was also widespread fear about what havoc the internet and the World Wide Web could cause. People feared for their jobs, doomsday scenarios were played out, and mass unemployment was forecast by the naysayers. Technology was a risk to employment, and people were wary.

However, as we now know looking back with hindsight, the internet and World Wide Web were not the technological doomsday scenarios people first imagined they would be. In fact, a study by McKinsey, published in

2011, actually found that the internet had been a catalyst for job creation with 2.6 new jobs being created for each job lost due to the technology. They also found that 75 per cent of the benefits of the technology were captured by non-technology companies, showing the vastly positive impact of this technology upon every sector and type of business. Their final finding was that the internet, in 2011, accounted for 3.4 per cent of gross domestic product, and 21 per cent of the gross domestic product growth over the prior five years could be accounted for by the internet and its technologies (Pélissié du Rausas et al, 2011).

Fortunately, we have moved on from Web 1.0, and cemented ourselves into Web 2.0, where we see multimedia coming to the fore. The Web in its 2.0 version became social, users had more interaction with the web and its websites. Users started to create content, and social media came to the fore. If Web 1.0 was a 'read only' model with the host generating and holding authority over content, Web 2.0 heralded the era of 'read–write' where users could generate content, but the host continued to have the authority.

But now, we are on the cusp of Web 3.0 which will, once again, send shock-waves through companies and their business models (as the Web becomes decentralized, and technologies such as distributed ledger technology take off, for example the blockchain). The naysayers may once again share a raft of concerns and reasons why the 3.0 version of the web is going to harm us, but there is no escaping the fact that technologies like artificial intelligence, virtual reality, artificial reality, and the Internet of Things (sensors) are converging and the world is about to fuse physical and virtual into one. Web 3.0 heralds the era of user-generated content, and importantly, user generated authority.

Our choice is the same as it always has been. We can choose to *run from this reality, or we can face the situation* in the best way possible and try to ensure we use the technological advances to our advantage. As the McKinsey study concluded, over ten years ago now, 'companies should pay attention to how quickly internet technologies can disrupt business models by radically changing markets and driving efficiencies' (Pélissié du Rausas et al, 2011). This advice remains as true today as it was then. Our culture and outlook will dictate what we do.

Embrace technology; do not run from it

One of my favourite images to show when making presentations is to put a photo of an automated teller machine (ATM) on the screen, and then ask the audience who has used one. Normally, 98 per cent of the people put their hand in the air; there are always a few people who haven't used an ATM, but the vast majority have interacted at least once with this technology. Well, much like the internet and the World Wide Web, when ATMs were first introduced in 1971 by banks there was a lot of scepticism. ATMs were thought to be a lower-cost way to serve customers compared to expensive bank branches full of employees. And, you guessed it, the general reaction was that these machines were here to replace people's jobs and their employment opportunities. And of course, yes, the ATMs were designed to serve customers at a fraction of the cost compared to traditional face-to-face banking, but they were also designed to allow people to bank in their own time, no longer constrained by the opening times of a branch. They were also there to help people when they needed money but there was a snowstorm and the branch couldn't open, and they were there to free up the time of bank staff who could then better use that time to help support customers with more complex queries.

As more routine transactions were handled by ATMs over the years you would have been led to believe that the number of branches would have reduced. However, in a study by David B Humphrey of Florida State University in the United States, he found that not only had the number of ATMs installed increased (from a low base, as expected) but the number of bank branches had expanded too. In fact, from 1973 to 1992 in the United States the number of branches expanded by 57 per cent, which was much faster than the 21 per cent growth seen in the adult population (Humphrey, 1994).

Data points from the International Monetary Fund and The World Bank suggest this phenomenon was not limited to the United States. In fact, if we look to more recent times we see the trend continuing, with 42.78 ATMs per 100,000 people in the world as of 2019, compared to 18.29 in 2004 (The World Bank, 2020a). And, with the number of bank branches at 11.51 per 100,000 people in 2019, compared to 9.79 in 2004 (The World Bank, 2020b).

So, why has this been the case? Well, ATMs and the technology behind them made simple transactions much more cost effective for the banks. The reduced costs of serving customers who wanted to do simple transactions such as balance cheques or make withdrawals of cash no longer needed manual intervention from an employee. As the bank staff had their time freed up as a result of the technology they could spend their time really dedicated to getting to know and help their customers. Customers were more satisfied, and branches became cheaper to run and operate, and thus technology had contributed to the boom in new branches and extra employment.

CASE STUDY
Gymshark

One of the most inspiring chief executive officers I spoke to during the research process for this book was Ben Francis. Ben is the co-founder and CEO of Gymshark, a company founded in 2012, which has been wildly successful in the design and manufacture of fitness apparel and accessories. In 2020 the company raised additional capital, valuing the firm at over £1 billion – their expansion plans see them aiming to become a truly iconic global brand that outlasts all of us.

Gymshark have fostered a very strong, positive internal culture. One which stands out and can really be felt when speaking with any of the almost 1,000 employees globally. They know that they are in a business where change is constant, be that market change, product change, structural change or people change. And their culture is founded upon the belief that they must be *'resilient through change, and open-minded'.*

On technology

Gymshark have a lovely relationship with technology, a partnership, it could be said. Of course, being founded in 2012 when social media was beginning to boom made them digital natives to a certain extent, but they have doubled down on digital technology. Digital technology is not only apparent in their logistics, warehouses and operations, but also in their marketing approach.

Ben shared with me that *'technological change is something that is going to continue, so you have to get used to it'.* And, as he navigates challenges around sustainability in manufacturing and distribution, materials innovation and a range of other challenges, technology is an enabler of solutions. Equally, in order to engage with customers, Gymshark has actively partnered with technology, and their creative agency has played a huge role in successful marketing campaigns. Ben says that within the company they are *'open minded'* about trying new technologies and *'the conversation isn't about should we do it, but rather let us try it and see what happens'.* A good example of this is their use of TikTok, the social media platform. Gymshark launched their TikTok page and had reached 1.1 million followers there before a single competitor had even opened their respective TikTok accounts. Equally, Ben shared that they probably tried *'three or four other social media platforms around the same time which failed'.*

On the future

A large part of the flourishing culture at Gymshark focuses on one of their 'core values', that of 'progression'. They say that 'Our products exist at the intersect of engineering and art. To remain at the forefront of both, we need to *be fearlessly progressive and consistently future-conscious'*.

Gymshark is building a Gymshark IQ building on its UK campus, and this building will host the technology, data and product teams, amongst others. Ben knows that 'if you were building the business purely for profitability and short-term growth, you would not build the IQ' but they 'want to *invest for the longer term'* and their focus on the future helps them innovate.

Technology is at the heart of the facility, with 'in-house sampling and production facilities' on-site so 'the designers and developers have the best chance possible to build our products'. Much like The LEGO Group, Gymshark knows that they need to *partner with the manufacturing process* so that they can design, build and test in a much more rapid manner than if their products were manufactured and outsourced across the world.

On mistakes

Ben says that '*in many ways, Gymshark is a story of failure'* as they *only began to taste success on their seventh website attempt*. Their first six website launches failed; they 'didn't get the attention we wanted, and kept failing and muddling our way through'. As such Ben takes the time to recount this story in his group meetings with all new joiners to the company, and in one-to-one meetings with any member of the team who asks him for time. He suggests that it is a powerful indication of the fact that their innovation and creative efforts must 'come from the ground up' and that 'people should be allowed to fail, in the best way, without reprimanding them for it'. Had Gymshark not learnt and continued to developed its technology, seven times in a row, they would not have had a sales funnel which has enabled them to reach over a quarter of a billion pounds of sales in 2020.

Their content production teams also make a play on this story, and other similar failures. Creating content for external viewers and their employees which really shares this, the Gymshark story. And as Ben says, 'the story really helps to reinforce their culture'.

On challenge

Finally, Ben shared with me the fact that he wants *challenge within the company to come not only from the ground up but also from the top down*. And, to that end, the team is assembling a Board of Directors that will be around five people, five experts in their fields, in the style of 'Avengers Assemble', which will challenge him and the team to be more innovative and push further. Their first addition to this Board is none other than Gary Vaynerchuk, who we saw at the start of this book, pushing his own companies and people to rethink their business models.

With Ben at the helm, and other innovation gurus such as Vaynerchuk on the Board, Gymshark stands a great chance of moving from apparel to becoming a leading fitness brand, as the culture of innovation is so powerful from all directions.

Fear

Of course, embracing technology and being as successful as Gymshark is in trying new things is easier said than done, and there are a number of pitfalls to watch out for. Fear is a common theme when people consider technology in the work environment. If we can overcome our fear of technology perhaps we can avoid the same misstep that Xerox made. Banks may have found a pleasing solution with their ATMs, but others have pushed back against implementing technologies at their own cost.

Xerox Holdings Corporation is a highly successful information technology company. They are famous and known around the world for their photocopiers, and their main business is printing and digital documentation products as of 2021. The company was founded in 1906 in New York, and spent its formative years manufacturing photography paper and machines. By 1958 they had invented the photocopier as we know it today, and their business revenues shot up to nearly $60 million in 1961 and then $500 million in 1965. The company went from strength to strength thanks to this wonderful invention.

The company continued to grow into the 1970s and 1980s and invested more money into research and development. At their research laboratory in Palo Alto, United States, engineers hit upon a potential goldmine. They created the Xerox Alto. The Xerox Alto was most probably the first personal computer. It wasn't basic, either. It was packed full of functionality, with Ethernet networking, graphical user interface, bit mapping, a mouse, and it was connected to the first laser printer ever invented.

Despite the fact that the Xerox Alto was an innovation that blew everything out of the water, and the engineers were jumping from the rooftops shouting about how great it was, Xerox did nothing with it. The executives at Xerox *passed up the opportunity to partner with this emerging technology*, which left the door wide open for competitors to come into the market and sweep up.

So, why did this happen? Well this was a good case of fear at play. Xerox's leaders were not willing to move their eyes away from the photocopier which was their existing gold mine. There was a *psychological block* within the leadership team, who cited any number of reasons not to launch and market the Alto or further invest in it, because they *didn't want to risk their existing business*, which was doing great.

It was a case of what could have been. Apple, Microsoft and IBM swept into the market and by the 1980s Apple had released the Macintosh personal computer – at that time, Xerox realized their mistake, but it was far too late.

If you are interested in learning more about this, a book published in 1988 by Douglas Smith and Robert Alexander titled *Fumbling the Future: How Xerox invented then ignored the first personal computer*, sheds more light on what went on inside Xerox (Smith and Alexander, 1988).

Leave your ego at the door

As well as the fear of technology replacing your job, or the fear of taking your eye away from your existing business lines, *ego also plays a massive role in stopping partnerships with technology*.

We can see this with hackney carriages in London, England. Hackney carriages, or black cabs as they are known, have been the envy of taxis across the world. To be a black cab driver, drivers have to pass a test which is called 'The Knowledge' to show that they have a very detailed and clear knowledge of every street in London, and that they know the main buildings, memorials and points of interest. The preparation for the test often involves drivers spending thousands of hours trawling the streets of London on mopeds studying maps attached to the front of their bikes, come rain and high winds.

Passengers can take one of the c. 14,000 black cabs in London (Mayor of London, 2021) and be assured that when they ask to be taken to a particular building or street, the driver will know the exact location and the best route. Which is a far cry from the local taxis in other towns and cities; until the early 2010s I often had to direct the driver, from the backseat of the taxi, to the destination as the driver simply didn't know where to go or how to get there, and certainly would not think to consult a paper map!

But then, along came the smartphone, and with that a range of apps (downloadable from the open innovation platform app stores) that would help you navigate from your starting point all the way to your destination. Apple Maps, Google Maps and the like.

In 2006 a start-up named Waze began operations in Israel, which incidentally is a hotbed for digital innovation. Waze offered users satellite navigation software free of charge, directing them and diverting them based upon prevailing traffic conditions. The Waze software is based upon crowdsourcing, the concept we have become familiar with in the previous chapter. Users report traffic-related incidents from accidents through to police speed traps, and their real-time traffic information helps Waze to navigate its users through the most appropriate roads. Users benefit from less traffic on their routes, faster journey times and reduced fuel costs as well as more carbon-efficient journeys. The app now counts on around 140 million monthly users and the network effect of so many users means much smarter driving routes for users than ever before.

Whilst Uber drivers drive around cities and towns worldwide using Waze to get their customers to their destination in the fastest and most economical manner possible, some of the black cab drivers in London seem to have been resisting the use of Waze and other similar apps since they first appeared on the scene. Why have they shunned its use? Why would anyone pass up the opportunity to have their passengers more satisfied as a result of faster and cheaper journeys? Why would anyone not like to increase their own revenue by having their taxi available for more customers, as opposed to sitting in traffic? Well, their egos have in no small part had an effect. These highly trained drivers, with street names engraved in their brains thanks to The Knowledge, have not wanted to partner with technology because they have felt that using mobile satellite systems to route them around London would be an admission of their weakness. There have been numerous examples of arguments between passengers sitting in the back of black cabs holding their phones in their hands and, for instance, telling the driver that the A13 road has a tailback due to an accident and there are twenty-minute delays, whilst the drive maintains that they have taken The Knowledge and the A13 is always the fastest route.

Avoid the sunk cost fallacy

So, if technology isn't taking our jobs, we are not scared of it, and we have checked our ego at the door, perhaps the final blocker we face culturally when trying to embrace new technology is the sunk cost fallacy.

A sunk cost is an economic term used in business when a company has already spent money that cannot be recovered. A sunk cost is different from a future cost, or a prospective cost, which is a cost that may be avoided in the future if action is taken.

Sunk costs are no longer relevant, economics argues, to decision making as they cannot be recovered. However, when people make decisions they often account for their previous expenditure and factor that into their decisions regarding future spend, because of human psychology. The fallacy effect is that people tend to continue with their line of action, their investment, their decisions because they have previously invested so much into it. People literally 'throw good money after bad'.

Both Kodak and Concorde fell into different variations of this fallacy when assessing new technologies.

Kodak

The Eastman Kodak Company (Kodak) is famous around the world, with its distinctive red and yellow logo, and its 'Kodak moment' strapline known by photography enthusiasts all over. Kodak started life in 1892 in New York, and focused on photography, holding the most dominant position in the photographic film market for much of the 20th century.

However, in the 1990s Kodak began to struggle, facing competition on a number of fronts from emerging technology – digital photography. Digital cameras were beginning to proliferate in the market and digital printing solutions were eating away at the traditional photographic film market. Kodak, however, had little by way of response and in January of 2012 filed for bankruptcy in New York. Since then, Kodak has made a mini revival, but the business remains a shadow of the past (Brown and Agrawal, 2013).

So, what happened to Kodak? Well, as they were making record profits and dominating the photographic film market, in 1975 a team from Kodak invented the first ever digital camera (Anthony, 2016). But, you guessed it, senior leaders at the time faced the sunk cost fallacy and *decided that their existing investments into photographic film had been so expensive and continued to eat precocious resources that they had to continue with them,* rather than switch and take the digital path.

Concorde

Kodak wasn't the only company to fall into the trap of the sunk cost fallacy.

The Concorde aeroplane was a revolution in passenger air travel. The plane was meant to usher in the era of supersonic travel for high society. It promised to travel at over twice the speed of sound, with a maximum speed of 1,350 miles per hour, meaning it could get to most destinations in less than half the time of any other aircraft (British Airways, 2021).

However, after taking its first flight in January 1976 the plane retired from service in October of 2003, having provided just twenty-seven years of flights at supersonic speeds, with only fourteen passenger jets in use, and a further six for non-commercial use. It was one of the lowest-selling aeroplanes in history. It wasn't a particularly bad plane, though there was a fatal crash and two other non-fatal incidents reported during its time in service; it was mostly just an expensive one. One that was in fact too expensive.

The British and French Governments continued to plough money into the development of the Concorde aeroplane, long after it was deemed non-commercially viable. The money they continued to put in to develop the aeroplane was so nonsensical that the Cambridge Dictionary includes the words 'Concorde fallacy' with a definition of 'the idea that you should continue to spend money on a project, product etc. in order not to waste the money or effort you have already put into it, which may lead to bad decisions' (Cambridge Dictionary, 2021).

The development budget for the Concorde aeroplane was estimated at the start of the project to be £70 million (which adjusted for inflation is £311 million in 2021 money). By the time the project eventually concluded the costs were £1.3 billion (£3.4 billion in today's money) (Pirie, 2019).

Neither government felt able to say 'stop' during the development process; they proceeded to fund the project because 'they had come too far' and 'spent too much money', despite knowing they would have to spend a whole lot more.

Culturally, we have to proceed with caution when assessing our business lines, the operations of our companies, and new technologies. Being aware of the sunk cost fallacy will help us to make smarter decisions in the face of psychological challenges.

Use technology to help you with your biggest challenges

Since 2020, the majority of office-based workers have found themselves no longer working in offices, though the re-balancing is certainly coming into effect now, as many migrate back to office spaces. As Covid-19 swept around the world in early 2020, whole countries went into national lockdowns, in order to protect the health of citizens and minimize the transmission of the deadly virus. Companies were presented with one of their biggest challenges yet: how to keep operating in the harshest of conditions. And, of course, they turned to technology to help them. As the CEO of Microsoft, Satya Nadella, said in April 2020, 'we have seen two years' worth of digital transformation in two months', and it was true: companies begun to digitalize at rates never seen before (Mari Tottoc, 2021).

Office workers found that they could work from home without problems, often enjoying an increased experience and satisfaction with their jobs now the roles were remote. Of course, burn-out and the nature of workers being connected 24/7 have created new issues people have had to face, though largely I find that these have been challenges particularly specific to working from home during a pandemic whilst having caring responsibilities, etc, occurring at the same time as work responsibilities; it does appear these issues are subsiding. People used Microsoft Teams and Zoom for video-conferencing, messaged one another using Slack, Yammer and Whatsapp, and collaborated on projects using Mural, Sharepoint, Office 365 and Google Docs. With smartphones in abundance, people had an office in their pocket and it worked. Those companies that had proactively prepared for such events were ahead of the curve and switched their employees to be remote workers overnight, and those who were a little more reactive followed soon after, quickly scaling their technological capability.

In addition, there are many non-Covid-19-related challenges that companies face, brought about by technology. Not least that the rapid technological changes are leading to skills shortages. The half-life of skills is becoming ever shorter, and training needs are increasing at companies across the world, as changing technology necessitates new skills. However, smart companies have begun to proactively partner and use technology as their secret weapon to combat the challenges that technology, ironically, induces.

Take virtual reality (VR) as an example. VR is the use of computer technology to create a simulated environment for people to enter into and engage with, and was one of the trends we commented upon in the introductory chapters. The VR market is well served, despite still being in its infancy, with headsets for users to wear over their eyes being sold in their millions. Popular brands include HTC Vive, Oculus by Meta and PlayStation VR. The visual, immersive world that these headsets encourage us into in fact can help boost our learning. So, as we need to learn more skills, on a more regular basis, without taking huge amounts of time away from the front line and costing companies an arm and a leg, turning to a new technology is actually proving very useful.

Take Walmart, for example. Walmart is a retail business, operating grocery stores and department stores mostly in North America, but with some world-wide presence. The company employees over 2.3 million people worldwide – their training budget is one of the largest in the world, and the complexity of keeping the skills of such a number of employees up to date is a challenge most human resources professionals would baulk at (Walmart, 2021). However, Walmart has pioneered the use of VR technology for training and development. Walmart knew that proactively investing in new technology would lead them to opportunities in the future, and they found that using VR headsets for training was a wonderful way to handle ever-changing development needs.

In Walmart Academies their employees use VR headsets to immerse themselves into real situations, in a virtual environment. They use the headsets to learn about what to do when shoppers rush into shops during the sales and fight over products, and they learn how to respond to angry customers, and well as test key management skills. They have noticed that not only is the training faster, with some training which may have previously taken 45 minutes to complete now being concluded in just five minutes within the virtual environment, they also find that test scores have increased by 5 to 10 per cent compared to traditional classroom-based methods of learning (Lewis, 2019). Millions of Walmart employees have had the chance to experience VR learning; the results are phenomenal and the company is delighted. They used technology to help with one of their biggest challenges and were successful.

And it is worth noting that Walmart isn't the only company taking steps to use VR for their challenges. This industry is on the cusp of explosion, with other companies such as Bell Helicopters using VR to design helicopters ten times faster than typical design methodologies, or fire-fighters using the FLAIM Trainer to tackle simulated blazes and hone their skills, or 3D4Medical, which uses VR to educate students and patients on the anatomy of the human body in detail never seen before.

Your value digitalized

But your VR capabilities should not be the only technological solution you look to for help.

Michael G Jacobides, the Sir Donald Gordon Chair of Entrepreneurship and Innovation and a Professor of Strategy at London Business School, co-authored a *Harvard Business Review* paper during the pandemic with Martin Reeves, the Chairman of Boston Consulting Group's BCG Henderson Institute in San Francisco, which discussed strategies for adapting businesses to face the new reality during and post-Covid-19. In their article, they noted that shops were posed with an unusual problem; because of the lockdowns, they had no customers visiting them. However, Lin Qingxuan, a natural cosmetics company based in Shanghai, China, *partnered with technology and transformed their business* in the hardest of times. Or, in the words of Michael and Martin, they '*digitalized their value*' (Jacobides and Reeves, 2020).

Upon closer inspection, Lin Qingxuan was faced with a 90 per cent collapse in store sales when lockdowns were first enforced, with very few stores across China remaining open, and those that remained open having a much lower footfall than was normal. The company had over 300 retail stores and employed more than 2,000 employees in those stores to look after and serve every customer need. The in-store service was a key differentiating factor for this cosmetics brand, which makes its products using traditional Chinese herbs as the raw materials.

Sensing that the company was in trouble, on 31 January 2020 the founder of Lin Qingxuan, Sun Laichun, wrote a letter to employees calling for their help and ideas on how to keep the business going. 'Partner with technology' was the response they got.

The executives at Lin Qingxuan quickly picked up the phone and engaged Ding Talk, which is a major provider of mobile workplaces – think video conferencing and communication solutions – and Taobao, an online shopping platform for consumer retail products. Both these two companies are owned by the Alibaba Group, which is the technology giant based in China, founded by Jack Ma, and worth north of $530 billion as of August 2021.

Lin Qingxuan worked with the teams at Ding Talk and Taobao to create a digital strategy which would see them replicate, as best they could, the in-store experience online. As Michael and Martin said, '(they) turned the company's in-store beauty advisers into online influencers'. Suddenly, the Lin Qingxuan shopping advisors began using their mobile devices to engage directly with customers using the Ding Talk platform, providing one-to-one advice and creating a large social media presence. As followers grew, Lin Qingxuan promoted their products and offered discount coupons to followers, who could place their orders directly using the Taobao platform.

Just two weeks after the call for solutions, Lin Qingxuan launched a targeted live-stream shopping event. With over 100 of their team members participating, and 60,000 people logged in to watch, they sold over 400,000 units of their product. To put this into comparison, a two-hour digital event had generated sales equivalent to that of four stores in a month.

Lin Qingxuan had partnered with technology. In this case it was do or die, but they made the decision. Sometimes, we need just a little push. If we can build this mentality into our culture, we will find these decisions more straightforward.

Michael and Martin closed their *Harvard Business Review* piece with sage advice, summarizing that '*Increasingly, a firm's competitive space will be determined by the platform it works with*'. Companies have to work with technology, they need to partner in order to innovate and create digital value – there will be dire consequences if they don't.

Proactive steps to take

Whilst there is nothing wrong with quickly embracing technology as it is needed (as with the case of Lin Qingxuan), it can make sense to take a proactive approach to technology management. The most innovative companies are doing this; they are planning for the long term, future-proofing their plans, and preparing for future expansion and growth well ahead of time. The good news is that there are a number of strategies you can build into your business, in order to promote this culture of innovation through new technology. For example:

1 *Sense, scout and research:*

- The market is changing so fast, so rapidly, that it is hard to stay on top of all the changes. Ask vendors to come and explain their new products to you on a regular basis.

- Or, if you are short of time, ask one of the top consultancy firms to present a summary to you.

- Even without these you may find public resources looking at 'top trends' in technology useful. For example, those from McKinsey titled 'The top trends in tech' are extremely useful (McKinsey Digital, 2021).

- Run regular customer insight sessions in the form of surveys or roundtables to understand what their views are on technology, and research their opinions and views. Consultancies or companies such as Ipsos MORI can help if you prefer not to launch the research activity from within.

2 *Discuss:*

o Perhaps consider holding technology-related board meetings, strategy committees, or even monthly meetings with your executive team dedicated to discussing the latest technology, and how it could be applied across the company. Set out a clear agenda, with clear ownership of who is responsible for presenting which topics and set aside time to have these discussions.

o Make it everyone's responsibility to consider new technology. This is not only the chief technology officer's domain; we are all responsible. If you are holding discussions with the board or executive committee, consider having the discussion led by a colleague who is not from the IT team.

o Visit and participate in trade events and conferences around innovative technologies. Begin to build your brand as an innovative, technology first company, and a number of opportunities will begin to present themselves to you: earn this credibility.

3 *Partner:*

o You may choose to partner with third parties from the technology industry, to explore whether there are new products or services you could offer jointly. For example, Renault, the automotive maker, has partnered with LG Corporation in order to offer their electric car drivers an intelligent infotainment service from their dashboard – coming to new vehicles in 2022 (LG, 2021).

o Partner with a consulting firm or technology company to undertake a deep dive, a root and branch review of your business (in terms of existing technology, and future technologies which may be applicable). We don't have all of the answers; recognizing that and appreciating external support is an important cultural mindset to foster.

4 *Experiment:*

o Experiments are often more important than expertise, and you can build an environment where experiments with technology can be undertaken. Give your technology teams a space to safely try new things with real customers, and seek their feedback. Take an 'incubator' approach, and reduce your enterprise risk. Scale what works.

○ Give your teams time to innovate and try new ideas. Of course, the most famous example of a company giving their employees time to work on other projects is Google and their 20 per cent time, where employees are encouraged to work on projects outside of the scope of their daily work (which was responsible for Gmail amongst other innovations). Focus your 20 per cent time on technology and its (potential) applications.

5 *Recruit:*

○ Recruit technology acumen to your board of directors. This is an important step, ensuring you have senior leadership which has a track record and understanding of new technology to support your teams. A Deloitte study carried out in 2017 found that high-performing S&P 500 companies were more likely (31 per cent) to have tech-savvy board members than lower-performing companies (just 17 per cent) (Deloitte Touche Tohmatsu, 2019).

Do you want to work as a team?

So, the final question for you is, *do you want to work as a team?* Will you partner with technology on your journey? If you can push aside your fear, and leave your ego at the door, partnerships can prove very fruitful when innovation is needed.

Technology isn't new; new technologies are, but technology overall is not. In the 1950s credit cards were invented, then this technology was combined with the World Wide Web, and in Web 2.0 people could shop online, but were afraid of inputting their credit card details on websites. We are now at a moment where people have cryptocurrency and buy digital assets, but many are too afraid to link their digital wallets to Web 3.0 pages. It is normal to be worried and nervous about new technology, as there are always traps to fall into. But if we work together with technology, partnering side by side, with it we can succeed.

The Queen's Gambit remains one of my favourite Netflix original series, and it led me to investigate the game of chess in more depth. I had not played chess and had very little understanding of the game before watching the series. Interestingly, when looking through the history of chess there was a moment in 1996 when Garry Kasparov, a grandmaster of chess and one of the most successful and pioneering players in history, played against a computer (IBM, 2021). IBM had developed a computer called Deep Blue, which was developed to win chess matches. And, indeed, in February 1996 it beat Garry Kasparov in the first game it played. However, it was a six-game match, and Kasparov won 4–2 in the end. IBM went away and worked a little more on the code, and in May 1997 there was a rematch and Deep Blue was a 3½–2½ victor this time around.

Since that point in 1997 the world of chess never looked the same. Computers have routinely beaten the best chess players in the world. The use of computers to beat humans in other games has continued since then, and clearly computing power and technology are a match for men and women. That said, what came next was even more curious. Players experimented with different formats of advanced chess, where computers or machines intervened in different moments. What became clear was that whilst computers can beat humans, when humans and computers worked together they could always beat another computer operating independently.

Will you work as a team?

QUESTIONS FOR REFLECTION

- What investments in technology have you been putting off and deferring to a later date because of fear?
- Are there any projects you currently have where the sunk cost fallacy is playing a part in their continuance?
- Which technology providers could you partner with?
- Do you have a use for VR in your company right now?
- Have you exploited social media for your company and yourself?
- Do you have technology committees, and employees who consider how new technology could future-proof your business?

In the next chapter we are going to explore recruitment, and the types of profiles we need to hire into our companies in order to keep the culture of innovation alive. We will look at how to hire the right people, the type of brand we should be sharing externally with the job market, and the benefits this can bring to your innovation efforts.

07

Hire well

Hire character, train skill.

PETER SCHUTZ, FORMER PRESIDENT AND CEO OF PORSCHE

As we move towards the end of the book we will divert our focus away from technology and back towards our people. The people and talent that fill our companies, and are the true bedrock of our innovation efforts. *Talent is the foundation any great company is built upon.* So in this chapter we are going to dive into culture in the recruitment process, and consider the most important attributes to take into account as you look to hire the right talent for your team or company.

A company where everyone is in step with the culture, rather than fighting against it, will always achieve greater success. We will learn that great talent, with individual skill, is not always the right talent – and it is more important to prioritize cultural aspects than the learned skills of individuals. We will see that in an ultra-competitive job market, job seekers and talent are looking to company culture as a differentiator, and that if you position your culture well in the market, people will want to join your cause.

A company can only be as good as its people

Companies are built by people, for people. So it stands to reason that a company can only be innovative if its people are inclined towards innovation, or a company can only be customer-focused if its people warm to others and truly care about the customers. Companies are collections of people, each possessing their own set of skills, which should be put to the best possible use in order to solve the customer's problem or need.

Having companies full of the right people, with the right skills, is very challenging. When we looked at Walmart in the previous chapter, we noted that the half-life of skills is shrinking on a daily basis. That is to say, the usefulness of skills that we learn have ever shorter cycles for putting them to good use. And Walmart, along with others, has to continually train and develop its people, in a near real-time basis.

It might even be argued that undertaking a four-year university course is no longer a good move, because the things you learn in the first year of the course are almost certainly outdated and the world will have moved on by the time you graduate. That is not necessarily entirely true, but it illustrates the difficulties of knowing what to learn and when. Indeed, when you embark on a university course, the non-technical skills you learn, or soft skills as they may be called, such as collaboration, teamwork, the ability to present, adaptation, etc. are more relevant today than ever before. And the most important ability of all, as I always point out to my own students, is the 'propensity to learn'.

Propensity to learn

The propensity to learn, or aptitude for learning, is a student's intense, natural inclination or preference to learn new things. Fortunately for me, the majority of students I teach at both undergraduate and master degree level have this propensity to learn, otherwise they wouldn't be in the class, but this isn't necessarily the case of every employee around the world. This ability is, however, critical in the modern world of work.

Gone are the days where you could be a 'company man' and sit behind your desk for your entire career, slowly working your way up the career ladder as a result of your boss or manager retiring. Slowly but surely you would rise through the ranks, and move your way up until it was time for you to retire, often with a gold-plated pension as a result of 40 or more years of service to the same employer.

Since the 2000s things have changed, and the job market has become more open. People have more mobility, there are more visible job adverts on the web, and platforms like LinkedIn have started to take hold. We see people jumping from one company to another, though often keeping to their lanes and staying in marketing if they were from marketing. People now may work in five or six different companies during their career.

However, the world is changing once again and we are *entering a very fragmented workspace*, with people, in particular millennials, not only having multiple jobs in different companies during their careers, but also having projects, tasks or gigs on the side of these jobs.

Even if you were to stay with the same company and in the same role for your career, *you wouldn't be able to avoid learning new skills in order to stay relevant*. Take farmers, for example. Each year that passes they are forced to learn new skills, techniques and methodologies. A farmer driving a tractor is still a farmer, just as a farmer from one hundred years ago was when using a horse – both are a farmer in name. They are, however, farmers with a whole different set of skills.

Your chances of securing the job of your dreams or even side hustle are increased if you can constantly learn and adapt to the changing skills market. And you can only do this if you are willing to learn and *have a true propensity to learn*.

Curiosity

The second most important aspect when hiring people to come and help push forwards innovation, is that of curiosity. Curiosity has been a recurring theme when speaking to business leaders and human resources (HR) experts from across the globe.

Curiosity is a key trait for innovation, whether it is Gary Vaynerchuk, who we met at the start of this book, who says 'when people lack curiosity, they dismiss new opportunities instead of taking the time to explore them' (Vaynerchuk, 2021), or Chris Rainey, of the 'HR Leaders' podcast who I quoted earlier when talking about employee resource groups and crowd-sourcing ideas, who shared with me a wonderful book, *The Curious Advantage* by Simon Brown, Garrick Jones and Paul Ashcroft (2020). The book explores the behaviour of curiosity, and reflects Brown's experience as Chief Learning Officer of Novartis, the global pharmaceutical company. Novartis have a culture based upon being 'inspired, curious, and unbossed' and Brown likens the need to be curious to that of an ant colony who need to continually seek their next meal. If an ant colony has found one food source in abundance, but waits to find alternatives until the day the food source is washed away by rain, they may not survive – and he has built this *culture of curiosity* within Novartis *to continue experimenting and innovating*, ensuring colleagues keep active, ask questions and always learn (Novartis, 2021).

Bruce Daisley, the former European Vice-President for Twitter, and now the host of the 'Eat, Sleep, Work, Repeat' podcast about workplace culture, echoed similar thoughts when we spoke. Bruce authored a wildly successful book about workplace cultures called *The Joy of Work* (2019) and shared with me that when he recruits, specifically looking to fill innovation roles, alongside the need to *be an optimist* ('because most ideas don't work'), he looks for someone who has curiosity at their core, 'someone with a track record of implementing creative ideas'. Bruce was inspired in this regard by a biographer called Walter Isaacson, who wrote about da Vinci, Franklin, Jobs and Einstein amongst others, and identified that in order to be a true innovator you had to be curious – and *reflect upon the questions that a five- or six-year-old have, and persist with that same level of curiosity and questioning until they find the answer.*

And finally, Enrique Rubio, of Hacking HR (one of the biggest HR communities in the world) reinforced these messages to me when he said the smart employers were looking to hire those who '*try to move outside of their boundaries*' and were not 'handcuffed to their seats' – meaning, finding people who asked questions, challenged assumptions, and found opportunity to manoeuvre within their space.

Getting your hiring right

The often-used management maxim about taking your time to make the right hire is very true. A mistake in the hiring process can prove extremely detrimental to yourself, your team and your company.

The market is hyper-competitive for talent right now in much of the world:

- There are *global labour shortages*, driven by reduced fertility rates in prior years (The World Bank, 2019) and an increase in retirements due to the Covid-19 pandemic and people close to retirement age taking the option of an earlier exit from the workforce (Fry, 2020).

- There is also a *surplus of open jobs*, driven by a faster post-Covid-19 pandemic recovery, the shift to greater focus on service jobs, and government stimulus activities (EMSI, 2021; Bersin, 2021).

- These shifts are also against the backdrop of *increased change*, and *uncertainty* in the world. As the impacts are seen following the pandemic, the uncertain economic cycle will continue for many years yet, with differencing levels of impact in different countries and economies. The speed of growth and rebound will drive uncertainty across a more global and hyper-connected workforce.

Given this backdrop, the employees who have the best and most in-demand skills are in the driving seat and hold the cards when it comes to choosing an employer. This leads to many people filling vacancies with whoever they can get, as fast as they can get people in through the door. And, of course, these kinds of rushed hires which don't end up fitting well with the company cause damage through the increased time it takes to manage them once they are inside the organization.

So, hiring carefully and considerately is always worth the effort. As well as checking whether people have the propensity to learn, amongst other abilities, we should also check whether they are aligned to our culture. This is perhaps one of the most important indicators of someone's future success in a company.

Hire for cultural contribution, not fit

As ever, the goal of hiring people is to fill your company with great skills, skills that can help your company to innovate. It means that you require a wide range of people, with different skills, different life experiences and a whole lot of diversity. The wider range you can attract to join you, the more points of inspiration your company will contain, and thus the more successful it is likely to be with its innovation efforts.

However, most companies when they think about this tend to hire people for what they call '*cultural fit*'. What they usually mean by this is a less than exact assessment as to whether or not the *person might fit in with the rest of the team*, whether they might have similar values or hobbies or if they could imagine socializing with this person.

When hiring managers think like this, things can go wrong very quickly. Companies suddenly tend to become a big homogenous mass of like people, with everyone dressing in the same style, eating at the same lunch spots and sharing the same jokes. And this is a risk to an innovative culture because all of a sudden there is a lack of diversity (Shellenbarger, 2019).

And actually, this is not uncommon. Psychology plays a big role. Because *we all have an unconscious bias* within ourselves, some more so than others. When hiring people we tend to hire people who look like us, speak like us, act like us and behave like we do. This is natural, because we all judge ourselves as high-performing individuals with excellent careers – so hiring someone who is similar should be a good move, logically. We also take comfort in hiring people who are similar to ourselves because it makes us feel safer; we will be able to talk about our hobbies together and not have to sit next to some strange person in the office who is interested in something other than football.

However, this isn't the ideal approach. A better approach would be to hire for 'cultural contribution', a subtle but important difference when compared to 'cultural fit'. By this I mean hiring people who naturally share the company's vision and also align to the values and behaviours but in addition considering the new employee through the lens of 'What can they offer to the culture moving forwards?' This subtle difference compared to 'cultural fit' means that we avoid hiring people who are homogeneous with one another, and instead we find new characters to join us on our company mission, ones that are aligned with our vision and culture but that will add to it in a good way. Ones that will add new views and opinions, and will bring something extra to the team, whilst respecting the company culture. This is important when it comes to innovation, as we know innovation thrives when teams are made of many skills, disciplines and lived experiences. The individual views and circumstances people bring to the table help to surface innovation. If we look only at their 'fit' in terms of would you like to socialize with them and if they are similar to you then we lose a lot of richness and opportunity.

There are three areas you can try to learn about someone during an interview process that will allow you to judge them fairly: their values, their abilities and their skills. We are all very different as individuals; as people we operate differently, independently, and have differing perspectives. That is to be respected and can be a very good thing when encouraging innovation.

- When it comes to *values*, these are a *deep-rooted beliefs* that a person might have. These beliefs motivate their behaviours. People are very protective of their beliefs, and more often than not these are set in stone and very unlikely to change. It is uncommon to find people working together successfully if they have vastly different belief systems.

- A person's *abilities* are their *ways of thinking and behaving*. For example, someone may possess common sense, another person may possess creativity. Someone may be ultra-caring and others may be dishonest. Like a person's beliefs, these abilities are unlikely to change, though it is possible with work that they can.

- A person's *skills* are their *learnt skills*. Have they learnt Spanish as a foreign language? Or have they learnt computer programming? These skills often change and evolve, and as we know, skills have a short half-life. Contrary to popular belief, it is possible for nearly everyone to learn nearly anything given enough dedication and effort.

During the interview process, it is important to probe all three of these areas to begin to build a picture of your candidates and prospective new colleagues. However, the *most important areas to focus on are a person's values and their abilities*, and less important are their skills. Skills are important, vital in fact – someone who cannot write code for software is unlikely to be able to hit the ground running on day one of a new job. However, having colleagues that are working towards your company's or team's goal in a cohesive and collaborative way with the rest of the team is more important.

If people are not on board with the fundamental elements of your culture, whatever they may be, then it is unlikely they will enjoy working in your environment, and it is unlikely you will enjoy having them in your environment. During the interview process you should be looking to understand what their values and abilities are, and matching those to your culture. If you have an innovative culture, you should be checking that the candidates are in sync with it; do they want to serve your customers in the way you wish to, do they thrive in environments where collaboration is key, do they enjoy taking risks? Irrespective of if they like your jokes or enjoy the same food as you, they may indeed be the right 'fit'.

One of the best quotes I have come across related to this was from Patrick Collison, the CEO and cofounder of Stripe, the payments processing company. In one interview he said that the questions of *what do you want the culture to be and who do you want to hire, are in various ways the exact same question*, as who you hire will shape your culture – and that is why it is so important (Y Combinator, 2017).

Gary Bolles, the author of *The Next Rules of Work* (2021), spoke with me during the course of researching this book and shared another example of the importance of hiring well when it comes to culture. He explained that Dustin Moskovitz, the co-founder of Asana (a workflow management tool) and previously Chief Technology Officer at Facebook, had been so impacted by the (negative aspects of) Facebook's culture that he 'spent two years planning the culture of Asana before it started' and 'intentionally thought about the cultural profile of who they were going to hire, before they hired a single person'.

Will the candidates add or subtract from your company culture?

Some great hiring practices

The cat is out of the bag for Southwest Airlines, but one of the techniques Southwest is famous for using is their method of checking on values before the formal interview starts.

Often, candidates need to fly into the headquarters of Southwest, which are in Texas, for the interview and thus they need to take a plane ride from their hometown. Southwest arranges the flight for the candidates and their journey begins.

Unbeknown to the candidates, the interview has already begun! As candidates wait at the boarding gate and then embark upon their journey, the ground crew and flight crew and watching and interacting with them, seeing how much they smile, whether they are respectful and pleasant, and whether they show an interest in Southwest's customer experience. *The crew then report back to the headquarters upon their values assessment.*

Other companies do similar – for example, they might observe how the candidate greeted and treated a chauffeur or the reception staff. A rude or curt first impression to the reception staff is normally a sign of things to come.

The second company with a great hiring practice is Disney. Disney also likes to look deep inside people and *consider their values and abilities*. They tend to ask probing questions, which shock candidates at first, like 'What was your dream job as a child?' or 'What do you dream about achieving in the future?' These questions find candidates searching inside themselves for their truths, and reveal an awful lot about their values.

EXAMPLE INTERVIEW QUESTIONS

1 Values

- Tell me about yourself.

- What motivates you to work at this company, in this role?

- What are you most proud of in your career, and why?

- What is your dream, and are you working on it?

- How do you perceive failure?

2 Abilities

- How do you like to collaborate?

- What factors do you consider when taking risks?

- Do you enjoy working in a group or individually, and why?

- What was your work ethic like as a teenager?

- Are you driven by learning new skills?

3 Skills

- My personal favourite, to check if someone has the skills they claim on their CV, is to ask them to do some 'homework' after the interview. Send them a short Excel or coding test, a PowerPoint to create, or a piece of writing. You will be able to understand far better than trying to question the skills in an interview.

Demand cultural compliance

Once you have hired a great team, you are well on the way to building or reinforcing the culture you want – for innovation this of course is team-work, speaking up, growth mindset, working with constraint, etc. However, you will also need to *demand* cultural compliance. What this means is that new hires, as well as all existing employees, *need to follow and align to the company culture*, because when people don't, disaster can strike.

Of course, when new people join, they bring different experiences and viewpoints, and that is good, welcomed even – especially for innovative cultures, their contribution is key. But this is your company, your culture and your way of doing business and you need to stick to it. You can expand your culture, as indeed I hope this book helps you to do, but this is a decision on your terms, not that of new hires. So, if someone joins and starts trying to remove transparency by failing to record meetings or share minutes, they may very well have a good reason for doing that which you should discuss with them, but *if it doesn't fit your culture then it needs to be nipped in the bud*. Cultural compliance is important.

We all know and have experienced meeting someone who is a great individual but has ruined or harmed the culture. That leader who gets fantastic business results, but shouts at people in meetings and makes them feel belittled. The damage that this person does to the culture and to the company is far greater than the stellar business performance (which is usually short-lived, and built on shaky and unstable foundations).

Imagine the case of a person who has called a meeting and takes the role of chairperson. This person has mandated that twenty people interrupt their daily schedules to come to a one-hour meeting, with pre-work undertaken. During the course of the meeting, the chairperson becomes rude, shouts at people and generally ruins the meeting with poor behaviour, feigning interest in the proceedings and, at the end of the session, the meeting concludes and participants see it as a complete waste of time. Indeed, the purpose of the meeting has long been forgotten and everyone moves on. Irrespective of the fact that the participants from the meeting may be harbouring bad feelings towards the chairperson and trust may have broken down because they have been shouted at (which is bad enough), the company has wasted well over twenty hours of resources on this one meeting, including the pre-work required. The cost of the meeting, and the interruptions to the attendees' normal day is significant. Yet, in many companies this kind of behaviour goes unchecked. This is in stark comparison to the person who sneaks into the stationary cupboard when no one is looking, towards the end of the day, and slips some pens, notepads and a calculator into their pocket. This act of theft, though bad and punishable with a criminal penalty, could be argued is less impactful to the company. Culturally, the person who has ruined the meeting has caused the company more distress than the thief. Yet the thief is normally punished, and the chairperson is not.

Great talent is not always the right talent

It is far more important to have people aligned to the culture, than people who are at the opposing end of the spectrum. A set of *people who gel well*, *work together*, and *align behind the same values*, will *always win* out *against a team of stars* who are smart individually, but mismatched and ineffective when it comes to working together.

It is a difficult but necessary step to remove someone from your team or company when you see they just don't click with the rest. The damage that will occur by keeping them and trying to have them change their values (which is nearly impossible to do) will harm those around them (and perhaps harm them too), and the kindest step is to let them go.

Previously I had lived in the North of England and enjoyed taking in football matches at various stadiums. One of the clubs I had a close affiliation to was Stockport County who play at a stadium called Edgeley Park. They are neither a huge club nor a small club, but they are certainly a club with rich history and fight in them.

In 2008 I went to watch Stockport take part in the play-off semi-final second leg against Wycombe Wanderers. Stockport won 1–0, having drawn 1–1 in the first leg in Wycombe, meaning they went on to face Rochdale in the final at Wembley to see who would be promoted into League One. In the end, Stockport won the final and gained promotion to the league above.

The match at Edgeley Park will live with me for ever. I can remember going on to the pitch with the fans after the game and celebrating their win, their chance to play at Wembley in the final. And what stuck with me in particular was a song that rang out around me. It went as follows: 'Jim Gannon, Stockport loves you more than you will know.' Jim Gannon was the Stockport manager. He had spent most of his playing career as a centre-half at Stockport and clocked up 383 appearances for the club. He then went on to manage them three times during his managerial career (this was the first spell).

I have followed the club ever since, and in January 2021 the fans at Edgeley Park were still singing the same song. Jim was, and is, a cult hero around those parts.

One story caught my eye. In his third spell as manager, Jim had helped Stockport gain another promotion, and then on 21 January 2021 he was sacked by the Board. It came as a shock, because at the time the performance on the pitch was excellent – Stockport were sitting in fourth place in the league, and looking to be on course for yet another promotion under the guidance of the cult hero.

Stockport's board simply stated that Jim had parted company with the club with '*the decision [not being] results based, but... centred around culture*' (Stockport County, 2021).

It appeared that even though Jim was a great talent, he wasn't the talent that the company needed. He was replaced with a coach who has a different philosophy for playing style and a willingness to use very cutting-edge methods for talent identification, player development and tactics. Stockport has chosen a culture change.

So, whilst it can be difficult to let people go, it is in the interests of everyone if it helps align the team or company around the culture you want and need to foster. Keeping those in roles who are against the culture is not worth it, even if they are a superstar cult hero.

Your external brand

The final element to consider when it comes to recruitment, hiring the right people to fit your culture, and weeding out those that don't fit, is what branding you have in the market. As we know, employees have the pick of the jobs at the moment. And thus it is vital that companies are a great place to work, and don't just offer the biggest salaries or best stock options, as people generally won't stay long in toxic cultures if that is all that is on offer.

TopResume, a leading resume writing firm, surveyed nearly 120,000 job seekers in 2020 and asked what the *top factor was for them when considering a new job*. Overwhelmingly '*company culture*' came out on top. Irrespective of who you ask, and what data you look for, the HR consultancies all say the same: for the past five years the importance of culture has been the most important, or one of the most important, focus for job seekers when considering who to work for.

What people see externally is important; it is an indicator of your culture, and will help or hinder your talent attraction efforts. Some good recent examples of companies promoting their cultures as a method of talent attraction are Microsoft, Netflix and IBM.

Microsoft was known for its culture of silos and Manu Cornet, a programmer and cartoonist working much of his life in Silicon Valley, made this culture somewhat famous when he published his cartoon about the organization charts of leading Silicon Valley companies. In the cartoon, reproduced in Figure 7.1, you can see guns being pointed at one part of Microsoft by the other; this image represented the silo mentality and internal frictions within Microsoft. What do you think was happening inside Microsoft for one team to be (metaphorically) pointing guns at another? Clearly, there was a breakdown in culture, and it was harming innovation; results showed that, and it

FIGURE 7.1 Organizational charts

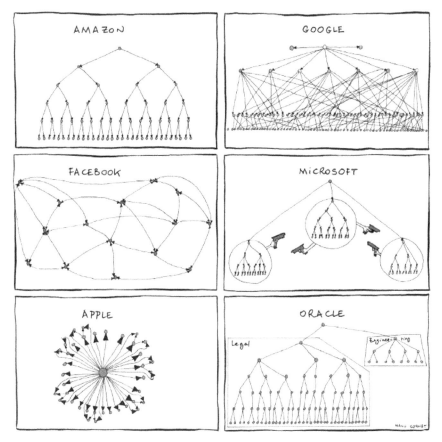

was clear to those inside the company that there was a lack of collaboration and teamwork (which, as we have already seen in an earlier chapter, is a key element for innovation to thrive).

As Satya Nadella took over at Microsoft in 2014, he made it his priority to turn the culture around. He even admitted in his autobiographical book of 2017, *Hit Refresh*, that the cartoon was one of the motivations for him to reinvent the culture. Microsoft have been on a journey of cultural transformation since Satya took over the leadership, and now are heralded as having one of the most progressive cultures. Their share price has jumped from around $40 when Satya took over (2014) to $336 in November 2021 (Yahoo Finance, 2021a). Culture has played a large part.

In 2009 Netflix released the Netflix Culture Deck (Netflix, 2021b), which very rapidly became an internet sensation. In this 129-slide blockbuster, Netflix published very explicitly for all the world to see what their culture was like. They set out their seven aspects of the culture and went through each one in painstaking detail. It let job seekers gain an insight into the working conditions at the company, and indeed it helped drive more and more people to apply for jobs at the ever-growing streaming giant.

As well as Microsoft and Netflix, Arvind Krishna, the Chairman and CEO of IBM, the technology multinational, shared its culture, or at least a very specific part of it, with the market in May 2020. Arvind posted on LinkedIn the 'IBM Work From Home Pledge' (Krishna, 2020). This document set out what IBM committed to doing in order to help make colleagues' lives more simple and easy as they transitioned to working from home as a result of the Covid-19 pandemic. It set out eight key areas of focus for IBMers (their employees) and stated that being in tune with family needs and personal needs was critical, as was being kind to yourself and one another, and ensuring digital disconnection.

But it isn't always about publishing your culture externally. It is also about *living the culture because it is the right thing to do*. In 2005 during the aftermath of Hurricane Katrina, Walmart used their logistics network and fleet of vehicles to deliver much-needed food to the community. During the Ebola crisis, Unilever provided 750,000 bottles of soap for washing, and the LVMH group during Covid-19 re-purposed their machinery to manufacture hand sanitizer.

We will see in the next chapter that it is important to value your people well, and look after them once they have joined the company; hiring well is just the first step. As well as allowing you to promote your culture externally, and try to control the narrative, the web makes it very easy for bad cultures to be shared publicly, and made an example of. So, you have to do what you say, and live by your culture, expecting any missteps to be uncovered.

With everyone on board, there is no stopping you.

QUESTIONS FOR REFLECTION

- What questions do you currently use to interview or get to know candidates?
- Are there any new questions you can incorporate around values and abilities?

- What are your own personal values and abilities?
- Is there any great talent in your team or company that is not aligned with the company culture?
- How do you position your culture externally? Do you have opportunities to do more?

Now you have the right people on board and in place, hopefully you will retain them and help them to unleash their full potential, tapping into all of their innovative passion and ideas. In order to do this, you have to value your human capital above everything else and build a culture where people come first. In the next chapter we will see that hiring the right people was the easy part. Giving them an environment where they can enjoy their work, feel respected and stick with you through the course will lead to more sustainable innovation. We will look at some practical steps you can take to boost the employee experience and create that culture of innovation.

08

Put your people first

Corporate culture matters. How management treats its people impacts everything, for better or for worse.

SIMON SINEK

In the penultimate chapter of principles, we are going to see that in order to have a sustainable, long-term, successful company you have to value your people above all else.

Innovation thrives when there is a great environment, where people want to come to work, and enjoy their work. Whilst we have looked at how to create innovation cultures, we also need to look at how to create good cultures, ones that help people to perform their best, and where people enjoy participating; if we have those conditions then innovation will thrive.

We will see that getting people to join your company was just the beginning of the journey, and that once you have filled your ranks with talent the hard work begins – you have to keep them happy and engaged in order to have great outcomes. By putting your people first, and making decisions in their best interests as individuals, you will find people begin to love what they are doing and cherish the environment they work in. When this happens, a company becomes unstoppable. However, you will have to continue listening to and acting on the feedback of employees as expectations always rise and the process of building a great culture and environment never ends.

Hiring was the easy part

Once you have hired your team, the hard work really begins as you now have to nurture them and give them the best possible environment. In the previous chapters you have seen how to build a culture where people can speak up and have their opinions heard, and we have also seen how to ensure a growth mindset filters through the organization – both of these will help you innovate. However, there are a few more things we need to do just yet before we can celebrate a great environment, and these kinds of things will ensure that innovation is really boosted.

Look after your people, so they can look after you

Many business leaders have said similar things to '*look after your people, so they can look after you*'. Richard Branson, the British entrepreneur responsible for the Virgin brand, has long said, '*Clients do not come first. Employees come first. If you take care of your employees, they will take care of the clients*' (Raymundo, 2014). J W Marriott, founder of the Marriott hotel chain, liked to remark, '*If you take care of your people, your people will take care of your customers, and the business will take care of itself*' (Marriott, 2021). The list of similar advice stretches far longer than my arm, and if so many business leaders are preaching this, perhaps we should take note.

It is my belief that typically there are four or five stakeholder groups a company needs to provide for:

- Its *people*: those who are employed by the company (directly, or indirectly as contractors, suppliers, etc).
- Its *customers* and *potential customers*: those people who use the products or services, or those who may do so in the future.
- Its *shareholders*: those who have invested money into the company and now have a direct stake in the organization.
- Its *communities*: those people and places where the company works.

These stakeholder groups are connected to one another in a virtuous cycle. The more you strengthen each part of the cycle, the more the other areas are also strengthened.

For example, if you have more engaged people, they will absolutely serve customers better, which will lead to more customers doing repeat business with you, which means you should experience larger profits and shareholders will be happier, leading to an increased likelihood that you can invest in, and give back to the communities you serve and operate in.

It stands to reason that if you have happier customers, you have a chance of higher profits. It makes sense that if you have higher profits, you can invest more resources in supporting the community. However, it is clear that this cycle starts from your people, your employees. Without them, the cycle would not stand a chance of working. And that is why you must put your people first.

The millennial interview

I was told a story a long time ago by a close friend of mine, and mentor, about what really happens when millennials go for an interview, and it was pure comedy gold with a very important punchline which I have remembered ever since. The story goes as follows:

A millennial has an interview at a company and they are waiting in the reception area to be called to the room where the interview is about to take place.

The hiring manager and human resources manager both arrive at reception and exchange pleasantries with the candidate before showing the millennial into the room. In the room there is a typical work desk, with a set of drawers underneath it and three chairs – two behind the desk, and one in front of the desk.

The hiring manager and human resources manager sit behind the desk and invite the millennial candidate to take the seat in front of the desk. The hiring manager opens the interview by saying to the candidate that today they are going to be asking a number of questions in order to assess and get to know the candidate, ultimately to decide whether the candidate will be a good fit for the job role which they have open and available.

The candidate is slightly surprised, and says that they understood an interview was a two-way process, and that they would like to ask the questions as well. To which the two managers reply that it would be fine for the millennial candidate to ask some questions, absolutely, because it was important that they get to know the company and its culture as well.

The interview starts and the two managers ask the millennial the first few basic questions. After this short period of time, the candidate has had enough and says that it is time that the table is turned and that the questions the millennial has are answered. The managers are taken back by this, but agree nevertheless.

The millennial asks their first question, which is 'Please can you tell me about how you manage flexible working arrangements, and how many days a week are employees required to be in the office.' The managers both smile, and the human resources manager says that the question is very easy and that they will share the answer. The human resources manager reaches into their jacket pocket and pulls out a key, reaches under the desk, and proceeds to unlock the set of drawers. They put their hand into the drawer and take out a big red A4 binder which is stacked full of sheets of paper. This massive binder, they say proudly, is the company handbook, and the answer to the question about flexible working arrangements is inside.

The human resources manager flips through the heavy binder, and finally settles upon page 324 of the binder and proceeds to read a few paragraphs of policy about flexible working. Smiling from ear to ear at the response, the human resources manager thinks it has been a job well done.

The millennial is less than impressed by this, as the answer is simply reading out a policy, rather than an explanation of what it is really like in practice to work in the company. So, the millennial says, 'OK, let me try one more time, I really want to understand the culture of this place, so could you perhaps explain to me how you handle things when people return to the office after maternity leave?'

This time, the hiring manager has a chance to reply. And, taking the heavy binder from in front of the human resources manager, the hiring manager proceeds to check the index to this massive lump of paperwork and find page 267, which has the details of the company maternity policy. Again, the answer is delivered the same way, a few paragraphs of the policy are read out.

Then, the interview comes to its natural conclusion following a few further questions in the typical way, from employer to candidate. At the end of the interview, the managers stand up and thank the millennial for taking part in the selection process, and insist that feedback on either a positive outcome with a job offer, or a negative one with someone else being chosen, will be shared within a few days.

The millennial stands up and shakes the hands of the two managers before saying that they too will be sharing feedback. This time, the feedback would be about the company, its recruitment process, and its culture, and that the reviews would be posted onto Facebook, Twitter, Instagram and LinkedIn.

The moral of this story is that, whilst *employers used to have the pick of the talent, it is now the other way around*, and with social media and the internet, talented candidates are no longer afraid to share their own opinions of companies with the rest of the world.

You are being watched

Just a few years ago, it would have been unheard of that a candidate would post feedback about a company on social media, and share their thoughts with the world in a very open way. Possibly, had they done this, they would be blacklisted from future employment opportunities with that company, and certainly recruitment agencies may have thought twice about putting them forward for other opportunities had they posted negative reviews. Now, though, everything has changed. It is clear that companies are being not only judged, but reported on by employees and prospective employees alike.

A wave of firms have sprung up over the past decade offering places for people to post their reviews on companies. You can visit Glassdoor (www.glassdoor.com), a website which allows you to review companies anonymously, or Indeed (www.indeed.com), and do the same.

As 2021 came around, Glassdoor had around 50 million individual reviews posted to their site, and were tracking over one million different companies around the world; the chances are your company appears on these websites (Glassdoor, 2021). Companies are ranked on the approval rating of the CEO, the likelihood of recommending the company as a place to work to a friend, and their culture. As well as numeric ratings employees, ex-employees and candidates can also leave written feedback about the culture, the recruitment process or any other process you can think of. Glassdoor also aggregates salary information, and lets users search and compare their salaries with those of other companies, whether by sector, location or other demographics.

If you haven't seen your own Glassdoor rating, it is worth keeping an eye on it, of course, with the hope that it is already great, or that you can improve it. But if your score is currently behind the curve, reading the comments will give you useful insight, and you can take some corrective action accordingly.

Millennials are the dominant generation in the workforce

We all know that millennials are the flavour of the day, and their needs or demands when it comes to the world of work have shocked many; they do tend to have a bad reputation. This group of colleagues is never far away from a sensational headline about needing bean bags to sit on, or a mission to save the planet. And whilst it is true that they sometimes rate office perks highly, the fact of the matter is they just want a great place to work and are not afraid to say it.

The workforce now comprises five different generations in many companies, and this can pose a challenge. It is a wonderful opportunity to take advantage of true generational diversity and seek the opinions of a diverse group. Often each group has its own specific set of 'power skills' and it is your job to make sure they are used in the best way possible. However, it also means that companies are trying to solve the needs of very different people through their human resources teams.

There are, however, two generations which are most predominant in the workforce at the moment:

- Millennials: born between 1981 and 1996, so they were aged 25 to 40 in 2021.
- Generation X: born between 1965 to 1980, so they were aged 41 to 56 in 2021.

Combined, these two groups account for over 70 per cent of the workforce. There are also 'Generation Z', the youngest of them all, 'Baby Boomers' aged between 57 and 75, and a small number of the 'Silent Generation' who are 76 and older.

Millennials have a slender lead in being the dominant group, with estimates putting their representation in the workforce anywhere from 35–40 per cent, with Generation X just behind (Fry, 2018).

But everyone expects a great work environment

It is not just millennials who demand a great place to work, logically. As the other generations have seen millennials demand, and receive, various benefits in the world of work, they too have asked for their distinct needs to be met.

Gina Pell, a technology entrepreneur, coined the term 'perennials' to describe 'an ever-blooming group of people of all ages, stripes and types who transcend stereotypes and make connections with each other and the world around them' (Pell, 2018). *Everyone wants to be taken care of*, people are under huge pressures as a result of the Covid-19 pandemic, the pace of change has never been so fast and will never be so slow again, people are working out how to manage the fatigue of being on video calls all day, the lines between family and work have become blurred, and there is often no longer a commute (which science has indicated is a good thing for your mental wellbeing).

All employees now have a voice, a voice which translates into a company's Glassdoor rating and which reflects the work environment, for better or for worse.

You can't compete with people who love what they are doing

Just as it is very hard to compete at a sport, or at piano, with someone who started to learn their craft at the age of two years old and practised over ten thousand hours, when you have just started and are a novice, *it is also very hard to compete in business with people that love what they do and are happy.*

Having fun at work is critical, and we need to build cultures that allow for fun to take place. Imagine the case of Southwest Airlines, who we have discussed previously. One of the reasons that Southwest is able to have such outstanding business results is because it had fun ingrained into its culture. A key business model innovation which Southwest led with was their ability to have their planes on the ground for no less than ten minutes before sending them on their way again. This was something in the region of a five times improvement on other plane companies, and this business model innovation meant they had fewer delays, they had their planes in the sky making money on a more regular basis, and they could pass lower air fares to their customers, leading to loyalty and repeated business.

However, turning a plane around in just ten minutes is no easy task. It requires the captains and pilots of the plane to chip in and help remove rubbish from the seats; it requires baggage handlers to do their very repetitive work ultra-fast, and ground crew to be in sync with all of the moving parts along the way. I don't know about you, but to me, lifting hundreds of pieces of luggage in a short space of time seems like very hard, tough work. And indeed, it is not for the fainthearted. Well, watching the people who undertake this mammoth effort, something becomes very clear – they are having fun. They are *driven by the challenge* to turn a plane around in ten minutes, *they appreciate each other, they understand their work is vital, and they have fun along the way.* This is by design, rather than accident, as Southwest promises all employees that from the day they join Southwest, until the day they leave, that they should 'demonstrate warrior spirit', 'show their servant's heart', 'deliver legendary customer service', and '*express a fun-loving attitude and embrace the Southwest family*'. The company then actively works to make this culture a reality.

How do you think the Glassdoor ratings on Southwest are?

Compare them to some stories I have heard during the Covid-19 pandemic about employers who have their people working from home, in remote offices, as a response to the pandemic. Some employers took the chance to install spy software onto the computers, to log and track every movement of their employees – to count the number of emails and meetings people were having. This doesn't sound like a very good culture to me, where there is no trust, no empowerment and colleagues are not treated as adults.

I would suggest that it is better to be the company that has a fun environ-ment, and trusts its employees rather than the one that doesn't. Glassdoor ratings that read 'My boss would not let me leave my chair to turn on the dishwasher until after 5pm, or answer the door for an Amazon delivery' probably are best avoided.

CASE STUDY
Pax8

If you ingrain fun into the workplace, you are much more likely to have great outcomes. Someone who lives this concept and idea is John Street, the Chief Executive Officer, Chairman and Founder of Pax8. John is a serial entrepreneur and has built numerous successful companies during his career. He has spent the last ten years working on building US-based company Pax8, which helps others buy, sell and manage their cloud solutions so they can achieve more.

Having spent time with John, it quickly became clear that he is a culture builder, and prioritizes culture above everything else at his companies – and it has served him well. You can't help but be reenergized after speaking with John. He has an unbelievable handle on culture and runs his businesses by always putting his people first: a true pioneer and inspiration.

On putting people first

John shared a story from his early career, when he worked in telecoms and built a wonderful company there. His partner in the venture, and business mentor, was a financial genius and the business grew fast and consistently. However, there was one thing that nagged at John, and that was another partner in the business always beating his own sales figures by just 1 per cent each quarter. The team that was beating him was chaotic and lacked consistency in its people, the staff were not happy and chaos reigned supreme. On John's side was a happy and motivated team, but 1 per cent behind in sales. John tried to influence the other partner to take care of their people, and invest in them, but the leader didn't agree. John saw that people mattered, and vowed to focus on culture forever.

'What I learnt really quickly was that all the companies that talk about customers coming first have got it backwards, and should be talking about employees coming first,' said John in our conversation. He explained that, logically, having happy employees leads to customers having terrific experiences as they have just dealt with staff that were happy, and he has made this mantra one of the cornerstones of everything he has built ever since.

John has even 'fired' customers, and says that 'some customers really are not good customers'. John has put his people first, and protected them from customers who were abusive and turning work into a bad experience. Prioritizing his people in this situation has shown his team that he is committed to them, and 'they find it comforting' to know that they will be supported and put first above revenue.

On the importance of culture

John knows that culture is the business. His focus, and that of the leadership team at Pax8, is that as they scale up past 1,000 employees and grow to 25,000 they protect their culture. Right now their culture is very strong, but as they move towards a public offering on the stock market they want to maintain it, not only because putting people first is the right thing to do, but because 'companies are being rewarded (by investors) for having a strong culture'.

At Pax8 they also recognize that culture protects companies when they make strategic errors. They know that 'you can do all kinds of strategic things well, but have it fall down because of a bad culture. However, on the other hand, you could make some strategic errors, but a strong culture can overcome those'.

On a fun environment

Much like Southwest Airlines, Pax8 go to great lengths to ensure people have fun at work, and a piece of their culture is simply that 'they are funny' says John. They have built large doses of humour into their work days; everything is designed 'to be personal'. When people first join Pax8 they are made 'to announce in front of everybody, a weird, interesting, fun fact about themselves'. This helps with innovation later down the line, as people get to know each other personally, and when you know everyone personally you can help them find the right place in the company. So, in high-growth companies like Pax8, where rotation is frequent, they can move the best and brightest talent around.

Their culture is based upon *people having fun*, and having an *environment when everyone is engaged* and coming into a workplace with a great culture which they enjoy, they will perform better.

On training

John started his career at Arthur Andersen, the accountancy firm. 'One of the great things I learned there was they were the best in the business at training' and because of this training, they were a talent magnet: it was part of their culture. So, at Pax8 *'we train people like crazy'* – they invest heavily in training their team and giving everyone a clear career development path. At Pax8 they know many people will eventually move on from the company and work elsewhere, and they hope that people remember that they cared about their employees, and when these same people become employees at other companies and become decision makers in the IT purchasing process, they will be very inclined to buy from Pax8.

On mistakes and speed

One of the most impactful things Pax8 has done to ensure innovation and an environment where people can contribute is that they have focused on having a high-trust environment.

Trust at Pax8 flows in all directions. Leaders give trust to their teams in abundance, and in return they receive the trust of their people. As John says, the leaders make an awful lot of strategic mistakes, but they have the permission to take corrective action and keep going.

For innovation this is critical, and within a scale-up like Pax8, which is constantly evolving, speed is of vital importance. The teams at Pax8 need to be able to take decisions quickly, without having everything fully verified and aligned – because by that point, you are going too slowly. Without an environment where people trust each other to make decisions and fix things when needed, failures can wear you down and you can quickly lose the support of the team. However, *'when you have the permission to make mistakes you can build a company, as people trust that you are not making mistakes because of egotism, but rather you are just trying lots of things'.*

On mergers and acquisitions

Pax8 has grown in recent times through acquisitions, and the first question they ask during the process of selecting targets is *'Does this company have a cultural contribution and coherence with ours?'*

Their two most recent acquisitions, in Holland and the UK, have proven successful because of the cultural alignment between the parties. The management teams and chief executive officers have remained in place, and committed to Pax8. The strong elements of the Dutch and British companies have been incorporated into Pax8, and the strong elements of Pax8 have passed in the opposite direction, leading to 'companies that together can scale to a much bigger level now' whilst the team 'has a fun environment and can enjoy their work'.

As we have seen with Southwest Airlines and Pax8, people want to work in environments which put them first, and where they can have fun. When you have happy people, you have a greater chance of innovation. Research from Culture Amp, a leading consultancy in the field of culture, has indicated that when people are engaged with their work environment nearly 80 per cent feel like they are able to nurture innovation, whereas only half of the least engaged people feel that (Croswell, 2021).

Listening to your people is of critical importance for leaders, in order to be able to understand and respond to their needs and thus create the best place to work. However, because we consider listening strategies, there are a few other elements that you can utilize in order to put your people first.

Recognition

What gets recognized gets repeated. Again, research has shown that recognition of good behaviours and practices leads to higher levels of engagement, which in turn help with your innovation efforts (Elfond, 2021).

Working in a company where your efforts are recognized and appreciated is important: it makes people feel valued. Often, recognition does not need to be expensive. We all know that sending someone to watch the World Cup Final or the tennis championship at Wimbledon is an expensive way of showing recognition for someone's efforts; however, you could:

- Say 'well done' in town halls, and other company-wide meetings.
- Take your team out to lunch to congratulate them.
- Give out non-monetary recognitions, such as trophies or certificates.
- Reward people with extra time off work, or 'special leave'.
- Use peer-to-peer recognition (so people recognize each other).
- Send 'thank you' emails.

Ensure people know how they contribute

Linked to how we recognize people is making sure they know what they should be doing. As we saw with the Gympass case study, it is very important that people are aligned with, and understand, the objectives of the company and how their work contributes to the successful achievement of that.

Gary Bolles told me that in the course of his research and his academic life, the most successful companies he has studied and worked with have *'had some type of commitment to having people understand their strategy, the company structure and organization, and people understood how their individual goals, which nowadays are often in the language of objectives and key results, are linked to the team and the company'*.

Having everyone know what success looks like, and knowing what part they play in it, is critical, as, especially in innovative companies where rapid realignment is needed (as we saw in the case of Pax8), people are more receptive to change when they know its purpose.

Inspire people with purpose

If you have built an environment where people have fun, and can contribute, there is probably one more important action to consider.

Research indicates that *people want to work for companies which have a strong purpose* – a strong reason for the company to exist, and what it wants to achieve. For example, '64 per cent of millennials won't take a job if their employee doesn't have a strong corporate social responsibility policy'; equally, 'Gen-Z is the first generation to prioritize purpose over salary' (Aziz, 2020).

Maybe you are inspired to work for one of these companies (Fond, 2020):

- *Tesla:* 'To accelerate the world's transition to sustainable energy.'
- *LinkedIn:* 'To connect the world's professionals to make them more productive and successful.'
- *PayPal:* 'To build the web's most convenient, secure, cost-effective payment solution.'
- *Nike:* 'Bring inspiration and innovation to every athlete in the world. If you have a body, you are an athlete.'
- *Patagonia:* 'Build the best product, cause no unnecessary harm, use business to inspire and implement solutions to the environmental crisis.'

At Art Blocks, which is a company headed up by the ever-impressive Erick Calderon, they have been busy enabling artists to produce programmable, on-demand, generative art that is stored immutably on the Ethereum blockchain. In Figure 8.1 you can see an example of one of my favourite pieces, a 'Scribbled Boundary' reproduced with permission of its creator, William Tan.

Art Blocks is a company at the cutting edge of the Web 3.0 movement and is at the epicentre of all of the disruptive technologies we saw at the start of this book. In conversation with Erick, he shared with me that since their November 2020 launch, and very quickly, they have grown to fifteen employees and doubled down on their efforts to 'enable artists to make a living, so many of them can quit their day jobs'. They have been highly successful in their efforts, as artblocks.io has enabled many artists to generate life-changing sums of money, with many raising in excess of $15 million of sales with just one release. As Erick tells me, 'Many artists would spend their whole life working for less than $3 million in sales and be considered successful'.

With such large sums of money moving around in this space, the whole team at Art Blocks quickly realized that *they had a social responsibility to give back and support their communities*. And, as such, they have 'built a culture of giving' and this clearly drives them. Before the end of December 2021, Art Blocks had facilitated around $45 million of charitable donations – simply mind-blowing success. Artists, when launching projects on the Art Blocks website, set a percentage of revenues to give to charity (which happens automatically through the blockchain), and Art Blocks boost these contributions even further, with their fees passed to charities that matter to them during specific campaigns.

You can feel this 'giving culture' and their purpose very clearly when you spend time in the Art Blocks world. In just a few short months they have reinforced an internal culture of giving and all of the employees feel and support this. Everyone is looking for ways to contribute, with regular opportunities to donate, run charitable campaigns, have the community vote on which charities receive funding etc. The culture is tangible.

Listen to the voice of your employees

As we have touched upon, there is a multitude of ways to foster a better working environment, and improve the culture of innovation in a company. If you build an environment where there is recognition, people align to the

FIGURE 8.1   Scribbled Boundaries #963

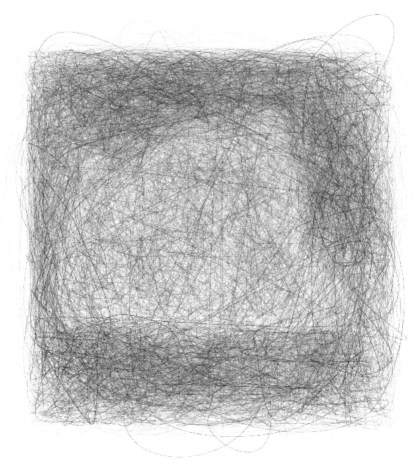

SOURCE   William Tan, Art Blocks Curated

purpose, and they have fun, you will be well on the way to having greater levels of engagement and thus better chances of innovation.

However, leaders don't have all of the answers – the people do. So, listening is critical. We have already seen that people love to provide anonymous external feedback on websites like Glassdoor and Indeed. As I say, I encourage you to check your online profiles and read the comments, in order to improve whatever it is that needs improving.

In addition to doing this, you should also be *listening to your employees on a regular basis*, using your own methods. Fortunately, with technology as advanced as it is, there are many ways to listen to your employees and understand their feedback that take hardly any time or effort at all. These technologies should always be augmented by having direct conversations with employees – nothing can beat an open and frank conversation. I recommend you *implement a strategy of 'continuous response and action'*, which means you are continuously listening, and always acting on the feedback.

If you have built a culture of growth mindset, as we saw earlier, and there is an abundance of psychological safety you will find that your listening activities are extremely fruitful, though even if this is something which is being improved upon and is in its infancy you will still gain rich insight from undertaking these kinds of activities.

At the heart of your continuous response and action strategy should sit your culture. You should aim to reinforce a culture of being able to speak up with safety, and that the company will take action, which is driven by feedback, assessment, data and experience, rather than by process.

You may choose to implement any number of these elements into your strategy:

1 *Pulse surveys*: A pulse survey is a short, and regular, set of questions sent to a rotating subset of employees.

2 *Annual surveys*: An annual survey is normally a longer survey than a pulse survey, utilized once a year or twice a year, with the set of questions sent to all employees.

3 *Crowdsourcing*: Crowdsourcing is a tool to gain feedback from a wide range of participants with the effort usually focused on a specific topic, and is highly interactive.

4 *External benchmarks*: External benchmarks normally take the form of a survey sent to employees, or are a set of questions responded to by the company about a specific topic, which are then analysed and compared to other companies and a rating or ranking is provided.

5 *360-degree feedback*: Feedback is given in a multi-directional manner (from manager to employee, from employee to manager, and from peer to peer), usually related to behavioural topics.

6 *Performance appraisals*: A performance appraisal is a regular review of an employee's work/job performance.

7 *Risk reporting*: Risk reporting may comprise of an analysis of whistleblowing channels, safety logs, near misses in the workplace etc.

8 *Incident reporting*: Incident reporting may comprise of an evaluation of all of the human resource or information technology incidents that have occurred in a given time period.

9 *Continuous feedback*: Continuous feedback is given on a regular basis, is multi-directional and relates to day-to-day experiences in the workplace.

10 *Exit interviews*: Exit interviews usually take the form of questions sent to those who are about to leave the company, to understand their motivations for the change.

The list could go on, but I am sure that you get the idea. If you use advanced reporting and analytics, sentiment analysis and network analysis you will have a very rich tapestry to work from when it comes to acting upon the direct feedback of your employees.

Employer of choice

It is absolutely critical that your company and your brand are associated with being an employer of choice for having a great culture and way of doing things. An employer of choice is one that people want to join and work with and for. Without this, you simply won't be able to attract the talent that is needed – in a highly competitive market globally, with major remote work shifts coming into play, it is only going to get harder and harder.

People are the only appreciating asset that your company has. The other assets, like plant and machinery, will depreciate with time. Take good care of your people, build their skills, knowledge and listen to their needs; they will pay you back in multiples of your investment.

Your people will be only too pleased to help you become an employer of choice, because it means their conditions and environment will improve. So, ask them, listen and act upon their feedback, and remember, money doesn't play well – the environment is the key: put your people first.

QUESTIONS FOR REFLECTION

- In what order do you currently put your people, customers/potential customers, shareholders and communities?
- What does your company's Glassdoor page look like?
- What kinds of actions are you taking to boost job satisfaction?
- What else can you be doing to improve the environment for employees?
- Do you take the time to listen to your employees? Have you asked them how the culture is?
- Are there any tools you are currently not using to listen to employee feedback that you could use?

In the next chapter we will consider the eighth and final principle for creating cultures of innovation. We will see that it's critical for leaders to be involved in the culture. If they are not then efforts to build the culture of innovation will fail. We will see some great examples and traits of leaders who really understand how to build such cultures of innovation, and we will close with a self-reflection to discover whether you are really committed enough to establishing a culture of innovation in your company.

09

Leaders, participate in culture

In the final chapter of principles, we close with a brief discussion of your roles as leaders in cultural transformation. As we saw at the start of this journey with the cultural web, there are many elements that contribute to a company's culture and many components that need to align in order to be successful.

In the introduction I posited that leadership has a large role to play, not only in setting the culture but also in changing the culture and living the culture for the better. If you want a true culture of innovation it must be led by leaders within the company. In this chapter we will explore what leaders can do to inspire action, what behaviours they must display and how to create the environment where a culture of innovation can thrive. At the very end of the chapter I ask you to reflect on how invested you are in your team or company culture, and whether you can do more. If you can find a way to do more, you will undoubtedly be rewarded with results far greater than any you may achieve with other management techniques. You will have found the culture advantage.

Culture is a leader's job

Every employee has a role to play when it comes to fostering, building and reinforcing a great culture. But there is no hiding from the fact that culture is a leader's job as much as anyone else.

Leadership is defined as 'the action of leading a group of people or an organization' (Virkus, 2009). To me, this means that leadership is really about influencing others, so that they do their best, in order to achieve a common goal, in this case for a company. As leadership is about influencing others, it means people need to lead by example, rather than lead by authority or diktat. As such, leaders have to be aware that their every move is being watched and replicated throughout the company. Each step they take quickly filters through to the front lines and people are looking to leaders for indications about the company culture.

This starts with the founding team and the CEO and filters down throughout the company. At board or CEO level, you are responsible for living the culture and enforcing the behaviours around innovation that you expect to see. If you don't, the culture will quickly break down. *As important as the actions are which you take, the ones you don't take are equally important and just as observed.* What we get is what we settle for – if you let bad behaviour go unchecked you are settling for a poor culture.

What is also relevant is that leaders do not just lead their own teams, they are responsible for anyone and everyone in the company – irrespective of reporting line. Especially so as, for innovation to thrive, inter-company boundaries and silos need to be minimized: research continually highlights the need for connectivity and cooperation across teams in order for ideas to spread. In this day and age more of us are leaders than ever before. If you run a project it is likely to be cross-departmental and you will need to lead members from outside your core team – this is the new reality (Bjerke and Johansson, 2015). And, finally, leaders always have the goal or outcome in mind. It is not influence for the sake of influence, but rather influence for the sake of a common outcome.

When we think about the cultural models from the start of the book, and all of the elements that are described, such as the stories, symbols, structures and power making, we can see that all of them are heavily influenced by leaders: for better, and for worse.

Great leaders

1. Are visible

Great leaders are visible within a company – they are people who are the role models. Take Sally Ride, for example. She was the first American woman in space. On 18 June 1983 she was just 32 years old when she travelled to space as a crew member on the Space Shuttle Challenger, flown by the National Aeronautics and Space Administration (NASA) in the United States. Whilst in space Sally controlled the robot which was used to deploy and retrieve satellites, and the mission was a success. In 1984 she took a second flight into space, before later leaving NASA.

Sally was the first American woman in space; two other women from the Soviet Union had gone before her. However, being the first female American in space brought her unheralded levels of fame and attention. Initially, Sally was not comfortable with this level of scrutiny and public spotlight, but after a while she grew to understand that she was indeed a role model and this was a very important responsibility.

Shortly before her death in 2012, she recorded a podcast interview with *Harvard Business Review* where she explained that young girls needed to see role models in whatever careers they might be, so that they could picture themselves doing those jobs someday in the future. She summarized that role models were vital because '*you can't be what you can't see*' (*Harvard Business Review*, 2012).

As Sally embraced her role in popular culture, she wrote books for children, and appeared on television shows and in songs. She received a number of awards and recognitions and even had two schools named after her in the United States. Sally Ride blazed a trail and was visible to young girls all across the United States. Since she retired from flight, another 49 females from America have travelled to space, and she continues to serve as an inspiration and role model to them and countless other young girls who have subsequently gone on to take roles at NASA or become involved in the study of physics, who otherwise would not have.

It is not just in the field of space where role models are important, of course. They are important irrespective of the industry. I am reminded of a video I watched in December of 2020. Leicester City Football Club unveiled their new training complex. The complex was a £100 million investment by the football club, and brought together all of their training facilities under one roof (Leicester City Football Club, 2020). What was most revealing was that Leicester City had decided it would be a good move to create 21 different playing surfaces (including 14 full-size pitches) for the teams to practise on. It made me think, why does one football team need 21 different places to play football on? They are just a squad of around 25 people and require one pitch at a time. What I found out, when digging a little deeper, was that the complex was to also become home to all of its academy programmes, which included all of the junior teams, the teams that sit below the main first team of the club. The facilities would see young footballers playing on the pitch next door to multi-millionaire superstars from the Leicester City first team. It would also see them changing in the same building, and sharing many of the facilities. The club also moved its administrative employees into the complex, so non-footballing staff would be close to the first-team players also.

This was a deliberate move by the football club, to have *everyone – irrespective of age or talent – under the same roof*. Their thinking, which is backed up by science, was that having visible role models in close proximity to their younger players would be beneficial. The young players would bump into and interact with the senior members of the team, and the visibility would also show the younger players that the superstar first-team players were people, like anyone else, who have perhaps lived on the same road as the younger players do now, they eat the same food and shop in the same shops as anyone else, and that they too can get the same success by following in their footsteps. Any myth about the top footballers being blessed with special genes or anything else will have been truly debunked.

The soundtrack to the video was 'The Times They Are A-Changin' by Fort Nowhere, a cover of the original Bob Dylan song – and it proved apt. Times at Leicester City certainly are changing, and young, aspiring footballers can only be helped by their closer proximity to successful, visible role models.

If we believe that visible actions are key for innovation to thrive, it stands to reason that as leaders you should consider what you can do to become more visible and encourage innovation. You may decide to try any of these ideas:

- Dedicate time to working across teams on a weekly basis.
- Encourage 'reverse-mentoring' where leaders are mentored by more junior colleagues.
- Double down on communication, and share knowledge about what is happening across the company.
- Make people aware of the risks you are taking, and share the learning when they don't go so well.

2. Inspire action

As well as being visible, leaders need to be able to inspire action. The best leaders inspire action by explaining 'why' first.

In the TED Talk 'How great leaders inspire action' by Simon Sinek (2009), he asks the question why Apple is so much more innovative as a company year in, year out than its competitors, despite everyone having access to the same pool of talent. He asks why Martin Luther King was chosen as the leader of the Civil Rights movement when there were other people, perhaps more qualified than him, to lead. And, why did the Wright brothers succeed in launching the first powered, sustained and controlled aeroplane flight in 1903, despite having a budget far less than the competition?

Sinek suggested that there was a common theme at play, and that in all of these examples, the leaders thought, acted and communicated in the same way as one another. Sinek posited that there was a 'golden circle' or 'why, how and what'. What you do, and how you do it, as a company is quite easy to explain. You could for instance make a great car, with the highest speed. Or, in the case of Apple, a great mobile communications device, that is simple to use. However, Sinek hypothesized that explaining what you do and how you do it is not exciting enough to inspire action, regardless of whether your mission is to convince people to buy your product, or to join your team and work with you on your project. However, those that start with the 'why' did inspire action.

If you can explain the why first, which is difficult, people will be inspired. If you can explain your purpose, your cause, your beliefs and the reason your company exists, or the reason you get out of bed in the morning, people are far more likely to be inspired. And when people are inspired by a purpose their drive is increased, which means more opportunity for innovation to thrive (Kaufman, 2011). And, in the case of Apple, it is clear to see they put the 'why' first. They position themselves so that they are challenging the status quo by making simple products, and thus they have a great mobile communications device. *As Sinek says, 'people buy why you do it, not what you do'.*

Martin Luther King is known for saying 'I have a dream', which is a clear display of personal connection and he shared his why with his followers. And it inspired massive action. Leaders have to influence their employees, which means inspiring them through the why. We have to follow those who lead because we want to, because we want to put our sweat and tears into the work, rather than because we have to, because we are working only for the monetary reward. Those who inspire others in the workplace will surely succeed.

If you want to inspire a culture of innovation, perhaps you should take the time to share your why – and set out a truly compelling vision of the future that you can achieve together: the team will figure out the what and the how. Or you could, in a crisis, try to inspire innovation by setting out why it's necessary (as your competitors close in) – though the former approach is likely to be more successful.

3. Set high, hard goals

The best leaders need to be able to *set high, hard goals*.

Most people are afraid to push boundaries. Think of the annual budget-setting cycle that takes place in most companies. It is something of an art form within companies. The finance team starts the process by sharing this year's budget and asking you to think about what can be achieved the following year. Of course, they are looking for an increase in the business results, and likely lower costs and increased revenues.

So, the dance starts. The business unit or owner reviews the budget and may submit a first version that is with a slightly smaller profit than the existing year, knowing that this won't be acceptable, and irrespective of what they submit they will have pushback when it comes to round two. They don't want to risk inflating the numbers at such an early stage, so they sit back and wait a few weeks before they are told this isn't good enough.

They share a second version, perhaps this time with a 5 per cent increase or small improvement on the previous year. Again, the finance team review it, and decide to impose a fixed 10 per cent improvement on the whole company's budgets irrespective.

This process can be self-defeating, as it allows for just incremental improvements year on year. It may also lead to people slowing down at year end if they have already achieved their goals, as they want to convert sales in January the following year, or not at all if it is likely to lead to harder-to-achieve budgets the following year.

So, we need leaders to be capable of setting high, hard goals. Especially when it comes to innovation, as most innovation efforts require a little magic and a big change, not just a 10 per cent increase.

This recommendation is founded on research from University of Toronto psychologist Gary Latham and University of Maryland's Edwin Locke. They discovered that goal setting is one of the easiest ways to boost performance and innovation. As long as the goals were 'difficult goals' they 'consistently led to higher performance' (Latham and Locke, 1991).

They found that *setting difficult goals boosted performance and productivity by between 11 and 25 per cent.* Their research found that in cases where goals were harder, people were found to be more committed to their goals, searched for better strategies in order to attain the goals, and responded more positively to feedback. People persist longer and put more effort into achieving high, hard goals (using more innovative strategies along the way). People are positively charged by such goals. That said, when setting such goals, it is also important to have a series of sub-goals that roll up into the overall goal, so people can reap the psychological benefits of boosting confidence through regular achievement.

In business there is one master of the high, hard goal, and that is Elon Musk. We have already seen how his ambition to make humans a multi-planetary species led to great success with the SpaceX rocket programme in a relatively short period of time. He is a great example of using high, hard goals in order to produce the highest levels of effort and performance, just as Latham and Locke proved. If we think back to the case of setting an annual budget, and keeping things more or less flat compared to the prior year, it is often the case that business as usual efforts bumble along, and in order for innovation to take hold we have to really push high, hard goals for the goals to cascade through a company. Otherwise, innovation is often thought of as someone else's job (De Jong et al, 2015).

The higher the goals, the higher the performance.

4. Create the conditions

Leaders need to be responsible for creating the conditions in which a culture can thrive; they are not responsible for doing the work or bringing the stories to life necessarily: that is the work of the team.

Much like the fantastic music conductors you can see at the Proms or when you watch an orchestra play, leaders need to create the environment and conditions for the musicians, or employees, to thrive.

Itay Talgam, an Israeli conductor turned business advisor, gave a TED Talk titled 'Lead like the great conductors' (Talgam, 2009). In this talk he shared a series of video clips from great conductors and studied what traits each of them were displaying. He related his findings back to leadership within a company, which he reasons is very similar to leadership within an orchestra.

Some of the conductors in the videos were serious, others were happy, some were feeling the pain of the music, and one remained with his eyes closed in a daze. Talgam said that the role of a conductor is to be an enabler, to enable the musicians to make their music, and interpret it how it needs to be interpreted. The musicians are the ones who bring a piece of music to life, not the conductor – and that was proven by the range of different conducting styles on display.

There was no micro-management, and no detailed instructions given to them on what and how to do something specifically. This resonates with me, as innovation is often non-linear, and there is no set of clear instructions on how to innovate and how to create; that has to be left up to those doing the innovating. The best piece of advice I can give leaders, to ensure this happens consistently in your business, is to *empower your teams to think and act on your toughest problems or challenges and then support them where they need or ask for support* (Fisher et al, 2021). Empower them by giving them the permission, resources and necessary approval to try things.

Indeed, the Harvard Business School Professor Francesca Gino has written a book called *Rebel Talent: Why it pays to break the rules at work and in life* (2018) and authored numerous papers which set out her hypothesis and research into innovation. And in these studies she has proven that people actually run into barriers and find that they are not empowered to make change happen, or to take risks. And thus empowerment is a core component for innovation, and she suggests that the *best thing a leader can do is to empower and get out of the way*: trust your teams and let them go, supporting as necessary.

Set the conditions, and leave the people to find their own way, using their intuition. A great leader is a partner to the employees, not a dictator.

5. Lead by example

Leading by example is absolutely fundamental to having a great culture of innovation. As we have seen, leaders are having their every move watched and reported on. Their behaviours are copied and replicated ten times over across companies. Their actions (and lack of) really do have a lasting effect. And this is why *leaders have to lead by example: not when they feel like it, but every day, consistently, without exception.*

When you lead by example, your actions create a picture of what is possible, or what is expected within a company. A story from Amazon, as they were starting out, illustrates this well.

In 1995, as Amazon was in its infancy, they needed some desks to work on. Their office was close to a hardware store and Jeff Bezos, the founder, and some employees went to choose their desks. As they were inside the hardware store they noticed that the price of desks was much higher than the price of doors, and so they made the decision to buy some doors, and affix legs to them – at a much lower cost than even the cheapest desk. As it happens Bezos was a better businessman than carpenter and the new desks often creaked, wobbled and swayed as the legs came loose, or were not perfectly in line with one another.

Jeff Bezos had set 'frugality' as one of the core values of Amazon, as he wanted to deliver value to the customer, rather than extract value from them. Frugality was key to this aim and through this small act of adding some legs to a door and creating a table, Bezos himself was leading by example and living the culture he had designed (Karlinsky and Stead, 2018).

As Amazon grew, these desks made out of doors have continued to feature in corporate offices across the world as a symbol of not only the frugality core to their culture, but also the ingenuity and creativity of Amazon. People who work for Amazon understand that these doors are part of the history and the culture of Amazon, and they serve as a reminder that Bezos was willing to lead by example and work from a rickety, unstable door-desk.

The other great example of a leader leading by example is Elon Musk. Musk is a colourful character by nature, but he really does lead by example. Musk is a very visible leader; he is on the shop floor working hand-in-hand with his employees. The proximity which his teams have with him is second to none, and he never asks someone to do something for the cause that he is not willing to do himself.

Musk has experienced the good times, like the sale of PayPal which made him a millionaire, and the bad times, such as his first divorce and being left on the edge of bankruptcy having invested all of his money into his companies. But he leads from the front, and despite running short on cash Musk has led by example not only by believing so passionately in his projects that he invested all of his money into them, but also by maintaining a singular focus on Tesla and SpaceX despite both facing enormous bills and challenges – challenges that would have broken most people.

With tight deadlines and massive pressure to deliver, Musk has proven to be a very hands-on CEO and one who is willing to get stuck in. At the Tesla factory in Fremont, Musk has been known to sleep either under his desk, or on the workshop floor in a tent, for days at a time. He has also done the same at SpaceX. He enjoys working a hundred hours a week, and whilst that isn't for most people (I would not judge anyone who gains pleasure from this activity) it does show that he is willing to lead by example and will always set the tone from the top.

In the case of Musk, it is also true that the culture at SpaceX is very intense and the engineers also work extremely long hours. They often last a few years before moving on to another less demanding job, but what is clear is that their boss doesn't expect them to do anything he wouldn't do.

If you are a business owner, you can't expect that your team love your company like you do. That is unrealistic, but irrespective of whether you are a business owner or leader within someone else's company, you can't expect others to do something if you won't do it yourself. If you want innovation, then start by taking the steps to innovation yourself. Go first.

6. Care about feelings

Zappos, the online shoes and clothing retailer based in Nevada, was founded in 1999 by Tony Hsieh. A little over ten years after founding the company, he sold it for $1.2 billion in 2009 to Amazon. One of the main reasons Zappos found massive success in such a short space of time was due to its culture. It was a culture that Hsieh had cultivated from day one. He had set out to create a company that would 'deliver happiness' and he achieved this aim through its ten core values, which were things like 'pursue growth and learning' and 'build open and honest relationships' (Hsieh, 2010).

He cared that his customers felt happy. He cared about their feelings, and their emotions. The same was true of his employees – he cared about their feelings too. He set out to build high-performing teams and promoted cook-outs, egg hunts, movie nights, bowling competitions, picnics, and even held massive parties at his house for all of the staff – he cared.

He became famous for saying that *'People may not remember exactly what you did or what you said, but they always remember how you made them feel, that's what matters the most'*. This mantra was a core belief at Zappos, and drove the company to its success.

Hsieh passed away in November 2020, tragically early, at the age of just 46. When he passed away, there was an outpouring from the culture community that I had not witnessed before. Here was a man who cared about the feelings of his employees and customers, and through the outpouring of grief it was clear to see that he had left a lasting impression.

Jürgen Klopp, the Liverpool Football Club manager, is a master of this art. Here we find another person, in a sporting context, who places a huge amount of value on the emotional side of things, and cares about the feelings of his team and staff. Klopp has mastered the human side of high performance.

A video circulated on the internet of the Liverpool players stretching in their homes, as Covid-19 caused a national lockdown. Klopp was seen greeting each player individually, as they joined the video call, with a very personal and warm greeting for each. He is seen saying happy birthday to one player (before then singing happy birthday), saying hello to the family of another, and laughing with others, all in multiple languages. This video, which leaked on the internet, was just one of many where Klopp can be seen saying hello to every member of staff in the football club, from the tea lady to the kitchen staff to the chief executive.

These small acts of care have set him apart, and helped Liverpool achieve sporting success. The players too have recognized that just deliberately 'saying hello' and caring about each of them individually have transformed a football club (Hunter, 2020).

Most people nowadays work in the knowledge economy, and our jobs require us to perform at peak mental state. We have to care for ourselves and others because our brains are just like an athlete who has a thigh strain and has to sit on the bench and recover – they need care and maintenance too.

All great leaders must care about people's feelings. Don't forget, as we saw at the start of this book, that the word culture comes from the Latin word *Cultus*, which translated means 'care'. It is true that how people make you feel, and how people treat you emotionally, leaves a strong impression. We often talk about someone's IQ (intelligence quotient), but their EQ (emotional quotient) is more important in leadership.

When you have truly caring leaders you are building an environment of psychological safety, which helps innovation to rise. Try to say 'hello' to as many people as you can today, and genuinely enquire about them: *show you care.*

7. Have certainty and positivity

Leaders should also be certain. Certain of their beliefs, certain of their direction of travel – and positive about their chances of achieving those beliefs.

Having a sense of self-assurance and self-esteem helps when being a leader, as you are likely to face many challenges, setbacks and tough days. Of course, I don't mean have blind faith, but a positive attitude and confidence in your work is critical. Innovation, and trying new things, is difficult. Whilst innovating, you face more setbacks than successes, so you need to stay positive as it's easy to become disheartened. If your people fall into disappointment and disillusionment then they will be far more likely to give up their innovation efforts.

Walt Disney is a wonderful example of a leader who had certainty and always maintained a positive outlook, despite hardships and troubles. It has widely been reported that *Walt Disney, of Disney fame, was turned down three hundred and two times by banks and investment houses* as he sought to get funding approved to build a Disney World theme park. On the three hundred and third time he was successful and now, as you know, Disney Worlds are phenomenally successful around the world. His employees who were working with him on the project remained fully supportive of his endeavours to seek funding, despite the rejections, as they saw a man who was certain of his dreams – and, in the end, the dreams came true (Asquith, 2019).

There are countless other cases of people gaining success just by being certain, despite others not agreeing – initially. The author *J K Rowling is another famous example of this. Her first draft of the Harry Potter manuscript was rejected no less than twelve times* by publishing houses. On the thirteenth occasion she found success, and was rewarded with seven best-selling fantasy novels, major movie licences, and massive merchandising sales. All of which have led her, as of 2021, to accumulate a net worth of £820 million, making her the 196th richest person in the United Kingdom (*The Sunday Times*, 2021). Quite a feat, and I for one am delighted that she never gave up in her quest to publish *Harry Potter*.

And finally, the last example of someone with a positive outlook and certainty in his product. Colonel Sanders, the founder of the fast food chain Kentucky Fried Chicken (KFC). *Colonel Sanders was 65 years old when he started KFC, and was turned down no less than one thousand and nine times in his quest to find a funder who liked his chicken recipe!* Over a thousand times rejected, but he was certain he had a sterling recipe to share with this world and kept at it. As of 2020, KFC counts on 24,104 officially licensed restaurants in all corners of the globe.

As a leader, you need certainty and a positive outlook, and you must transmit that to those around you, so they don't give up on their efforts to innovate at the first hurdle or setback.

8. Are truly empathetic

Empathy is a leader's super-skill or super-power. Empathy is the ability to understand and share the feelings of another and doing this as a leader will set you apart.

Daniel Goleman, the author and science journalist, set out what he calls 'the empathy triad' and explains that there are three different types of empathy, all important for a leader (*Harvard Business Review*, 2017).

First there is 'cognitive empathy'. This is where someone has 'the ability to understand another person's perspective'. By having cognitive empathy leaders think about the feelings of others and it means that in discussions they can understand the other person's view in a better way.

The second type of empathy is 'emotional empathy', where someone has 'the ability to feel what some else feels'. When someone displays emotional empathy, they use phrases such as 'I feel your pain' and they truly do feel the pain of the other person.

And the third type of empathy is that of 'empathetic concern', which is where someone has 'the ability to sense what another person needs from you'. This occurs when you already know what your wife or child is about to ask you, or a doctor knows your next question about the course of treatment they have just prescribed.

Having any, and preferably all, of these types of *empathy skills can help leaders to foster a culture that is more supportive and productive*. Research from the Centre for Creative Leadership has found that 'empathy in the workplace is positively related to job performance' (Gentry et al, 2007).

One leader who delivered a masterclass in empathy, and leadership in general, during the Covid-19 pandemic was the CEO of the hotel group Marriott, Arne Sorenson. Sadly, Arne Sorenson passed away, due to pancreatic cancer, in February 2021 and the world has missed an opportunity to continue learning from one of the greatest and most empathetic leaders it has ever seen, but if you watch on YouTube a five-minute video titled 'A message to Marriott International associates from President and CEO Arne Sorenson' you will find those five minutes very well spent indeed (Sorenson,

2020). In this video, Sorenson shares an update on the impact that Covid-19 is having on the hotel group. The video was published on 20 March 2020, very early in the stages of the pandemic, and especially so in the United States, where Sorenson and Marriott are based.

As you watch the video you will see that Sorenson is displaying many of the characteristics we have just seen above, like caring about feelings, being positive, being visible and leading by example, but most of all he is empathetic. He starts by saying many people in the company didn't want him to make this video, because he was sporting a bald head. He says this hairstyle, or lack of hair, is an expected result of the pancreatic cancer treatment he has been having, and there is nothing unusual about it. He is not worried about his own appearance, nor is he concerned with the appearance of the video, which has clearly been made at short notice, and is a cheap and easy-to-produce video with poor audio-visual qualities (which is quite uncommon for leaders).

He signals his emotional empathy immediately by sending his best wishes and sympathies to those affected by Covid-19 so far. He shares that he understands and feels the pressures, highlighting his empathetic concern, and as he proceeds, he makes a number of mistakes with his speech (which were not re-recorded), his voice trembles and he shows his vulnerability – he talks from personal experience.

As he continues, he injects positivity about 'overcoming the crisis we face' into a speech filled with uncertainty. He treats everyone as adults and does not sugar-coat anything. He is clear, this is a difficult time.

He leads by example and explains that he has forgone his salary for 2020, along with his executive team who are taking a 50 per cent reduction in pay. Tears begin to fill his eyes when he says that there is 'nothing worse than telling highly valued associates that their roles are being impacted by events outside of their control' and you can see that he is deeply emotionally involved.

Of course, Sorenson shared this video because he is a great leader who needed and wanted to communicate to all of his employees in their time of need, not because he wanted to show the world how empathetic he was – but for students of empathy, or leadership, this video is a must watch. And whilst we will not have the chance to reflect upon his learning as the CEO of Marriott through an autobiography or masterclass, due to his untimely death, we do have this important video to reflect upon.

Both what Goleman sets out in his research, and what we can see from Sorenson, show or indicate to us that empathy in leaders is a critical business skill. However, going deeper, and again referencing the research from the Centre for Creative Leadership, empathy is clearly shown to help people work together more effectively. Empathy is proven to support the 'creation of shared direction, alignment, and commitment between social groups' (Gentry et al, 2007). So now you can see the link between empathy and collaboration. Leaders need to be empathetic to ensure their teams work well, and collaborate across organizational and cultural boundaries, so they drive innovation.

There are many other characteristics and traits that it is important for leaders to embrace. But when it comes to building culture, and in particular cultures of innovation, these are the eight which stand out to me, being repeatedly seen across successful companies and in academic research.

CASE STUDY
WD-40 Company

Garry Ridge, as CEO and Chairman of the WD-40 Company, presides over a company worth $3.15 billion with a presence in 187 countries worldwide, whilst counting on a workforce of over 500 people (Yahoo Finance, 2021c; WD-40 Company, 2021). You have probably used their products to help lubricate, degrease, clean, or protect against rust in your home or on your car. If you haven't, certainly the mechanics you have come into contact with will have. The distinct red, blue and yellow WD-40 cans can be found in all good hardware stores globally. However, the relevant and impressive part of this is that Garry has built the company based upon culture. In his own words, *'we truly believe that culture is a competitive advantage'.*

   Garry is perhaps the most enthusiastic person I have come across when it comes to culture, and I was truly blessed to spend time with him discussing the secret recipe to the success of the WD-40 Company. We covered many topics, and it's clear that WD-40 Company is innovating according to many of the principles set out in this book, but when it comes to leadership they really stand out as a class above the rest.

   During our time together, Garry explained to me that in the previous months, during the Covid-19 crisis, culture had become even more important. Garry noted that companies were *not suffering from 'the great resignation, but rather the great escape', as people are escaping from cultures* that don't fit them. People are leaving employers who have toxic cultures and are breaking free from them in search for employers who care about culture. His view is that one of the *biggest desires a human being has is to belong*. He suggests that most people will have experienced a time when they left a party, an event, a company, or maybe even a relationship, because they didn't feel like they belonged there. He posits that *people leave companies because they don't feel like they belong.*

And this is where WD-40 Company sets itself apart. *Apart from their secret formula for their product, their other secret formula is the will of their people.* At WD-40 Company they believe that if you have a high will among your people, then there's a chance that you will have a positive execution of your strategy. But if you have a low will, then the chances of you successfully executing it are much lower, irrespective of how good your strategy is. For example, using a scale of 1 to 100 for both strategy and will, if your strategy is scored 50 but you have only 10 in the will of the people, you get 50 x 10 = 500. However, if you have a strategy of 50 and a will of 50 you get 50 x 50 = 2,500: a big difference.

So, in order to create a place where people belong and have a strong will, they have built a culture around the concept of the tribe.

The WD-40 Company tribal culture

The WD-40 Company tribal culture is founded upon various pillars, which Garry explained to me.

1. Learning

The first pillar is learning, which is especially relevant to innovation. Garry says that *'innovation is about curiosity, the willingness to take a risk, and the ability to go through continuous learning'.*

And this willingness to be curious, take risk and learn is actually where the name WD-40 comes from. Water displacement, number 40. The team at WD-40 Company took 40 attempts to create their magic formula, the one we all know and love. And, the number 40 is testament to their origin. Had they given up in 1953 at attempt 26 it is true that Garry and I may never have crossed paths. Garry reminded me that this is why at WD-40 Company they say *'we don't make mistakes, we have learning moments, because a learning moment is a positive or negative outcome of any situation that can be openly and freely shared to benefit all people'.*

Within their tribal theme, when they considered what the responsibility of leaders would be, they identified that in order to have belonging as well as innovation, they needed their tribal leaders to create an environment where *learning is richly respected* and the *leaders are expected to be learners and teachers.* This is a sentiment that has percolated throughout the company.

2. Values

'The second thing that's important in tribes is you have to have a set of values. And values to us are not constrictive. They're freedom. They set people free'. The values at

WD-40 Company give people the permission to act, which is vital when it comes to innovation: the key is not to stifle decision making. At WD-40 Company the values are so well engrained that people *'can make any decision [they] want at any level in the company, as long as [they] use our values as the guideposts to making that decision'.*

The company has six values that direct and guide their tribe:

1   We value doing the right thing.

2   We value creating positive, lasting memories in all our relationships.

3   We value making it better than it is today.

4   We value succeeding as a tribe while excelling as individuals.

5   We value owning it and passionately acting on it.

6   We value sustaining the WD-40 Company economy.

Leaders are, literally, getting out of the way.

3. Belonging

The next attribute of a tribe is *belonging*. As Garry said when we started our conversation, people seek belonging. And it is true, according to the Maslow Hierarchy of Needs, that once people are safe and can survive they look for love and belonging. This is where WD-40 Company sets itself apart from many, as most people 'only know they are doing a good job because no one yelled at them today', as both Garry and the author Ken Blanchard say. However, in WD-40 Company leaders practice and *promote empathy, instead of ego*.

Garry suggests that 'in great cultures where culture is a competitive advantage, *people's empathy eats their ego instead of the ego eating the empathy'*. Leaders in WD-40 Company are expected to *avoid micro-management*, but instead they are expected to *coach and help the team*. They say 'we're not here to mark your paper, we're here to help you get an A'. Their job is to help the team get an A.

Garry thinks that micro-management is so damaging because the toxic behaviour of micro-management is driven by a leader's need to have their ego fed: by not having transparency, failing to have clear expectations. However when this equation is turned the other way, and leaders lead with empathy, they understand their *role is to set very clear expectations* and *then help people achieve them* (using the six values to guide their decision making and actions) – you suddenly have an environment where people are empowered (which is critical for innovation) and people feel belonging because they are empowered to make decisions without the need to ask permission.

4. Future focused

Then the next part of a tribe that's important is that it is *future focused*. This is where innovation really comes to the fore within WD-40 Company. Garry took inspiration from his homeland of Australia, and considered the tribes thousands of years ago. They had to think of the future, otherwise they may not have survived. They needed to plan for the fact that their lake may dry up due to prevailing weather conditions out of their control; they needed to know how to replace their food and water source, plan for the future. WD-40 Company has this very culture from top to bottom. They *'are looking at what beliefs they have today that could change in the future'*. Leaders have to promote this environment, where people are always tackling assumptions and scanning for new opportunities.

5. Specialized skills

As well as thinking about the future, and challenging assumptions – as we saw in Chapter 2 about rethinking your business model – the tribe knows that everyone has to contribute.

Garry learned from tribal leaders in Fiji and the surrounding islands that everyone has specific, specialized skills. Some people are naturally better fishermen, and others better hunters. There are better house builders, and better succession planners – each has their own attributes. The key within a tribal culture is to respect and appreciate this, and build a team where everyone is willing to *'come together to protect and feed each other'*.

WD-40 Company creates this environment by focusing on their just cause, which is to *'make life better at home and at work for our end users and our stakeholders in every avenue of our business'*. A compelling cause to come together and fight for, supplemented by leaders who appreciate everyone's unique skills and support them to achieve.

6. Celebration

And finally, *tribalism is about celebration*. Garry says that *'we celebrate in good times, and we celebrate in times that aren't so good because we're grateful for what we have'*. This time for reflection and celebration, together as a team, is vital for the tribe. And these actions reinforce the culture. Leaders celebrate alongside the whole tribe.

Challenges

However, setting up and implementing this tribal culture doesn't mean there are no speed bumps in the road.

The company likes to describe culture through the use of an equation:

$$\text{culture} = (\text{values} + \text{behaviour}) \times \text{consistency}$$

This simple equation is a description or a guide as to how you can build a culture within a company. We have discussed the six values of WD-40 Company and understand their behaviours – the tribal behaviours, and sense of belonging within the company. So now, the conversation turns to consistency.

All *leaders in WD-40 Company have to be brave*. Leaders have to be brave enough and love their tribe enough to not only reward the behaviour that really is aligned with the values, but to redirect the behaviour when it is not as needed. Garry says that 'in culture, if you're not consistently watching it develop, and you allow toxins to enter the culture without removing them, the culture will turn sour'. So, being brave enough as a leader to take action is expected in WD-40 Company.

Garry likened it to a high school experiment he had in Australia as a child. In science class, the teacher gave the students a Petri dish and said that they were going to grow a culture in it. The students' job was to know what went into the culture, and if they saw toxins entering the dish they were to either treat them or remove them. Because, if they didn't, at the end of the experiment the students would have a Petri dish full of toxic culture. This experiment and thought has lived long with Garry, and leaders are asked in WD-40 Company to manage the Petri dish of the company culture, consistently.

They ask their leaders about this. If there are some things that are reacting the wrong way, how do you treat them? How do you redirect the wrong behaviour? How do you make sure the values are in play? And if you can't fix that, how do you get it out of there? Because if you don't, the whole Petri dish will go sour. In the case of WD-40 Company they have managed their Petri dish meticulously, so they avoid a scenario where people are escaping a toxic culture.

So, how should toxins be treated or removed? Well, at WD-40 Company they believe that because there are well-defined expectations around each other (because they have worked on belonging and setting clear expectations) and six very clear values that drive everything, they can have solid conversations when needed. If people don't align with the values or expectations there is content to discuss, and leaders hold these discussions with the upmost fairness and transparency. For example, someone in a meeting hasn't created a positive, lasting memory and instead has been toxic in their behaviour. Leaders have an option; they can either ignore the behaviour, which means you are allowing that behaviour to continue (intentionally or unintentionally), or they can reprimand the individual for it, which probably creates an uncomfortable situation, or they can acknowledge it and have a conversation about it.

At WD-40 Company they value these conversations. Continuing with the meeting example, a leader may ask the person to speak and say, 'I noticed in the meeting you were not living our values, is everything OK? The you I know and love was not in that room just now, and I know you always live and uphold our values – what is on your mind?' With this kind of evidence-based, disarming conversation, you may get to the root of the issue and find the person had been in a traffic jam, or spilled their coffee on their clothes – whatever it may be. Then, the leader and tribe member will find the learning moment, reflect and move on. *'You redirect the behaviour through conversations, about a clearly defined set of values that everyone agreed to'.*

However, in instances where the values continually are not upheld it is time to remove the bad element before it sours the whole culture. Garry and the team use a lovely expression in these cases as they 'share the person with a competitor', meaning they help to find them a new role elsewhere, with respect and love. And in these cases, when people are not living the values, and only 'visiting' them from time to time, you find that they are not usually happy – so an exit with dignity is best for all parties. *Leaders have to be brave at WD-40 Company, because leaving a toxin in the culture is doing more and more damage to the company than can be imagined.*

It's not about you

Reflecting upon conversations with Garry, and learning more about the WD-40 Company culture has been one of the most rewarding parts of writing this book. Garry left me with one last bit of wisdom to pass to you, the reader. At WD-40 Company 'it's not about you, as a leader or individual. It's about how you create a place where people go to work every day, they make a contribution to something bigger than themselves, they learn something new, they feel safe, and are set free by a compelling set of values, and go home happy'. That's what WD-40 Company and its culture is about.

Culture cannot be outsourced to someone else. As a leader, it is your job. Are you focused enough on culture?

We have now looked at the eight principles for creating a culture of innovation and our journey is coming to an end. We will now move into the final chapter, where we have a chance to recap all of the principles in one place and take a look at a company that is one of the most innovative in the world, and which deploys all of the eight principles.

QUESTIONS FOR REFLECTION

- Is building culture a priority for you?
- How much time have you spent on culture-related activities in the past months?
- How often do you speak about the culture you desire, and share this with your teams?
- Are you visible enough when it comes to your company culture?
- How often do you challenge people when they are not following the culture?
- How much of the culture work do you subcontract to others?
- Do you set high, hard goals for your teams?
- Do you say hello to everyone you come across and truly ask (and care about) how people are really doing?
- Do you deploy enough empathy in your day-to-day interactions with employees?

10

Closing

When a flower doesn't bloom, you fix the environment in which it grows, not the flower.

In this, the closing chapter, we will recap the eight core principles and take in a case study from Shenzhen, China – we will explore the Chinese giant Ping An, who put each of these eight core principles to use in their quest for innovation, and as a result have built an unstoppable culture of innovation from within.

Recap

Having looked at companies of various shapes and sizes, hopefully by now you will see that it really doesn't matter your size, your financial firepower, how many people you employ or where you are located – innovation is within the reach of everyone, as long as you have the right culture (coupled with the correct strategy and execution of course).

We have taken in a journey that has seen us dart from Europe, to the United States, and into China. We have seen examples of start-ups and examples of large incumbent companies transforming themselves through innovation, and we have seen others who have had less success and passed up opportunities to change as a result of their non-innovative cultures and beliefs.

Eight core principles have arisen from this journey across multiple industries and sectors. And to recap, I list them here once again:

EIGHT PRINCIPLES FOR A CULTURE OF INNOVATION

1 Rethink your business model.

2 Create creativity with constraints.

3 Have a growth mindset.

4 Use the wisdom of crowds.

5 Embrace technology.

6 Hire well.

7 Put your people first.

8 Leaders, participate in culture.

These eight principles, if implemented consistently in your company, will help you achieve the innovation advantage. So, in closing, I wish to share one last example of an innovative company, one with phenomenal success, and one which takes elements from all eight of these principles and puts them to good use.

Ping An

Ping An Insurance, or Ping An as it is most commonly known, is a conglomerate operation in the fields of insurance, financial services, healthcare, vehicles and smart homes and cities.

A relatively young company, it was founded in 1988 by Ma Mingzhe, or Peter Ma to give him his Western name, in Shenzhen. The company has grown quickly, taking advantage of the headwinds of growth within China, and raced to a market value of $138 billion, entering the final months of 2021 (Ycharts, 2021).

Ping An means 'safe and well' and started its life as an insurer in the fields of property and casualty insurance: the type of insurance cover that protects you and the property you own (Bloomberg Markets, 2019). Typically, their policies focused on home insurance, car insurance, landlord insurance and the like.

Over time it has expanded, growing its business, and moving into different industries – thanks to its culture, which fosters innovation. For example, in 2014 Ping An founded Ping An Good Doctor, which is a healthcare platform. The company was formed as a result of a customer need and technological advancements.

Firstly, the customer need: the Chinese needed a better access point or route to primary healthcare, as there is no system of general practitioners or primary healthcare providers in the country. Instead, if you have a cold, a cut or a broken bone you have to travel to a major hospital to be seen. This means the sight of 50 people queuing outside a hospital at 4am waiting for it to open later in the morning is not uncommon, as people travel from the towns and villages into cities in order to seek medical advice – they are rewarded with queues. Once they find themselves at the front of the queue they are seen, often in as little as three-minute consultations, and sent on their way.

Secondly, the technology: China had 970 million smartphone users as of 2020 (Slotta, 2021b), making it the country with the most smartphones in the world. With around 1.1 billion adults in China it means the vast majority of the country has access to a smartphone in one form or another (World Population Review, 2021). And, the users are very trusting of technology, happily giving up their personal data and interacting with new technology via mobile devices.

So, Ping An Good Doctor was formed. It is a mobile app that connects patients with doctors of all specialities. Over 400 million patients make one million daily interactions with a network of tens of thousands of doctors in over 7,000 different medical centres and hospitals across the country (PR Newswire, 2021). Users can have a face-to-face discussion with a doctor, a text conversation, or in the cases where results need to be analysed, artificial intelligence can make the diagnosis, having looked at the results. The system leads to solutions being provided to the patient within 26 seconds on average. If medicine is needed, that can be delivered within an hour to your home or office location.

Ping An Good Doctor is incorporating the Internet of Things technology into its offering and blood pressure readings or heart rate monitoring from other devices are now supported, providing doctors with real-time patient insight and data. This phenomenal success led Ping An to list the company on the Hong Kong stock exchange – raising $1.12 billion (Reuters, 2018) – just four years after its founding, at a valuation of $5 billion, making it the most valuable health technology company at the time.

Good Doctor certainly was good business for Ping An. But how did an insurance company move into healthcare, and find a way to dominate it? Much of their success comes down to culture.

They rethink their business model

Ping An has never been afraid to rethink its business model. As we saw with Netflix, who rethought their business model and moved from DVDs by post, to streaming of movies, and now into production, Ping An has had the same mindset.

As the dominant force in insurance, Ping An may very well have rested on its laurels. However, in 2013, in a surprise move, they partnered with Alibaba and Tencent to co-found ZhongAn Insurance. The surprise was that Alibaba and Tencent were two of its main competitors, and in forming the first fully online insurance company the rivals became partners, but they also started to cannibalize and eat their existing insurance businesses. The level of vision and risk appetite, and willingness to rethink their business model, was astounding, and the insurance giant now counts 460 million customers, and has underwritten 5.8 billion insurance policies (Fisk, 2021).

They create creativity with constraints

As a company, Ping An has always been willing to build creativity with constraints. An important part of their business DNA has been that when they launch a new business line or venture they do it with start-up-like restrictions. This means they have small budgets, and they work with small teams in fast-paced sprints. Ping An now counts thirty-two successful individual subsidiary companies, and of these, thirty were created organically, using in-house resources. Just two of the companies were bought or invested into (Azhar, 2021).

As well as their self-imposed constraints, in China speed is always important. Speed is critical, much more so than in Europe or the Americas. The market is so large and there is so much competition, the first to market often wins out initially.

They have a growth mindset

These kinds of constraints were imposed by the founder Ma Mingzhe, who also makes sure the company has a growth mindset. He can often be heard saying that Ping An has two choices – to continue doing what they are currently doing or realize that they are living and operating in a changing world, a world where they have to accept that change is the only constant. As such, Mingzhe launched the Global Voyager Fund to ensure that Ping An was and is constantly scanning the market and understanding new, growth-stage technologies. The fund has $1 billion to invest, and has deployed just over $300 million of that capital so far, learning about the changing world as they go, understanding that nothing ever stays still in business (Wang, 2020).

Within Ping An they have spent time explaining that risk taking is strongly encouraged and failure isn't stigmatized. The founder says, 'You don't have to worry about failing at all. We just need you to try really hard to find a way to make it work. As long as one of these ideas eventually works, we'll be successful' (McKinsey & Company, 2018).

They use the wisdom of crowds

Ping An has deliberately focused on having a bottom-up culture of feedback. They describe their bottom-up culture as enabling everyone to share their ideas (EFMA, 2021). They are using the wisdom of their crowd, and those on the frontline who deal with clients and customers every day are highlighting pain points for improvement on a real-time basis to ensure that Ping An not only finds the next big innovation that drastically shifts their business models, but also undertakes the incremental innovations which are so critical in a market like China, where customer orientation is critical (Deloitte Touche Tohmatsu, 2014).

They embrace technology

At Ping An they are acutely aware of the need to partner with technology. In fact, in 2008 the company made its first pivot and Mingzhe led the change to Ping An becoming a technology-first company, with their entire operations becoming cloud based (Yu and Feng, 2020). Ping An uses technology as a fundamental enabler, and their in-house technology team builds solutions centrally that are exported across all of their business lines for their use. They believe in building the technology in-house, and as of 2020 Ping An employed direct just over 360,000 employees, with one-third of them in jobs related to technology (Slotta, 2021a).

They hire well

One of the most interesting practices that Ping An deploys is around hiring, and they do indeed hire well (*The Economist*, 2020). They hire aligned, taking into account the potential cultural contribution of employees. As we have seen, Ping An is constantly building new businesses, they fill these new business with a mix of internal employees who are moving from one project or one company to the next, and they recruit the best talent they can find from the marketplace. As each of their new ventures is run as a start-up, the new managers entering into the companies are expected to buy stock in the new company, which of course could make them very wealthy in the long term, but also ensures that they are fully aligned to the company goals, ways of operating, and culture.

They put their people first

Ping An is known for looking after its people. Not only does it count 360,000 direct employees, it also has a network of around 1.2 million life insurance agents who have direct relationships with their customers, and act as an offline distribution system (Olano, 2020). As Ping An has a long-term, growth mindset, it knows that its people are key to making the innovations come to life. Often the new businesses and ground-breaking business innovations have a long lead time, up to five years before they come to fruition. They support their people so that they stay with company during the whole business development lifecycle, ultimately making Ping An better off through the continuity.

And, their leaders participate in culture

Not only is Ma Mingzhe still a very hands-on founder, being deeply involved in everything that is happening across the Ping An empire, he also brings with him a very strong 'founder mentality'. He is the one that drives the business change and indicates that organic business creation, utilization of technology and start-up mentality (as examples) are the way things are done around there.

In the start-ups, because cost is tightly controlled – just like it would be in any other start-up – no managers or executives travel in first class; they keep to their shoestring budget and travel in economy. This is a great example of leaders living the culture, and a fantastic symbol for those watching.

Mingzhe is close to the employees, a visible leader. And the rest of his team live by the cultural rules and norms as well. The team sets very aggressive targets, following the approach of high, hard goals – and their people are galvanized by these (McKinsey & Company, 2018).

As you can see, Ping An at the moment appears to be an unstoppable force, with 598 million customers as of December 2020 (Ping An, 2021). They have time and time again changed their shape, changed their modus operandi, and continued to garner new customers and win market share, Undoubtedly their growth has been helped by favourable market conditions – they have a clear innovation strategy which sees them follow disruptive and structural innovations. Equally, they organize themselves in a very agile manner, with their start-ups and then their centralized technology functions (Greeven et al, 2019). However, above all, they follow the eight cultural principles for innovation. And, have spent thirty years deeply embedding these into the DNA of the company, they score highly on culture on the external ranking websites like Glassdoor (Nasdaq, 2021). Ping An will be a force to be reckoned with in the years to come.

Closing

I hope that you have been inspired by the stories in this book and that you will see that, whilst culture is difficult to change – very difficult in fact – it is always worth the effort. The investment you make in your culture will pay you back many times over, for better or for worse, depending on the culture you create.

There is no guarantee of success, and no recipe to copy. This is your competitive advantage in the end – culture cannot be copied like for like, it is what makes your company unique. However, these eight principles will see you, when well implemented, take a giant step forwards in innovation.

This is the culture advantage.

VIDEO RESOURCES FOR INQUISITIVE MINDS AND FURTHER LEARNING

Eames Office – *Powers of Ten* (1977)
www.youtube.com/watch?v=0fKBhvDjuy0

Sumatra Ghoshal – *The Smell of the Place* (1995)
www.youtube.com/watch?v=YgrD7yJwxAM

Leicester City – *New World-Class Training Ground* (2020)
www.youtube.com/watch?v=CvZDP7N2uQc

President Obama – *Fired Up! Ready to Go!* (2016)
www.youtube.com/watch?v=5AhRqgOADbk

The Pixar Story – Documentary directed, produced and written by Leslie Iwerks
    (2007)
Arne Sorenson – *COVID-19: A message to Marriott International Associates* (2020)
www.youtube.com/watch?v=SprFgoU6aOO

SpaceX – *Starship SN9 Explodes* (2021)
www.youtube.com/watch?v=49D3Sdxc61M

Simon Sinek – *TED Talk: How great leaders inspire action* (2009)
www.ted.com/talks/simon_sinek_how_great_leaders_inspire_
    action?language=en

Itay Talgam – *TED Talk: Lead like the great conductors* (2009)
www.ted.com/talks/itay_talgam_lead_like_the_great_conductors?language=en

REFERENCES

Afuah, A (2014) *Business Model Innovation: Concepts, analysis, and Cases*, Routledge, New York City

Alexa Internet (2021) The top 500 sites on the web, www.alexa.com/topsites (archived at https://perma.cc/2EHZ-55RK)

Anthony, S (2016) Kodak's downfall wasn't about technology, *Harvard Business Review*, 15 July, https://hbr.org/2016/07/kodaks-downfall-wasnt-about-technology (archived at https://perma.cc/5HHM-7CWE)

Anthony, S, Cobban, P, Nair, R and Painchaud, N (2019) Breaking down the barriers to innovation, *Harvard Business Review*, November–December, https://hbr.org/2019/11/breaking-down-the-barriers-to-innovation (archived at https://perma.cc/9Q3U-XCS8)

Ash, A (2020) The rise and fall of Blockbuster and how it's surviving with just one store left, Business Insider, 12 August, www.businessinsider.com/the-rise-and-fall-of-blockbuster-video-streaming-2020-1 (archived at https://perma.cc/Z8JM-5YQR)

Asquith, J (2019) Did you know Walt Disney was rejected 300 times for Mickey Mouse and his theme park, Forbes, 29 December, www.forbes.com/sites/jamesasquith/2020/12/29/did-you-know-walt-disney-was-rejected-300-times-for-mickey-mouse-and-his-theme-park/ (archived at https://perma.cc/HAP9-5L3P)

Azhar, A (2021) From insurance giant to tech platform: The story of Ping An: Chief Innovation Officer Jonathan Larsen explains how the Chinese conglomerate manages agility at immense scale, *Harvard Business Review*, 10 February, https://hbr.org/podcast/2021/02/from-insurance-giant-to-tech-platform-the-story-of-ping-an (archived at https://perma.cc/TZH2-D3KJ)

Aziz, A (2020) The power of purpose: The business case for purpose, Forbes, 7 March, www.forbes.com/sites/afdhelaziz/2020/03/07/the-power-of-purpose-the-business-case-for-purpose-all-the-data-you-were-looking-for-pt-2/ (archived at https://perma.cc/7LG3-KA5C)

Bailey, S and Black, O (2014) *Mind Gym: Achieve more by thinking differently*, HarperOne, New York City

Bayer (2020) *Annual Report 2020*, www.bayer.com/sites/default/files/2021-02/Bayer-Annual-Report-2020.pdf (archived at https://perma.cc/YVB4-NAZ5)

BBC News (2017) Uber founder Travis Kalanick resigns after months of turmoil, 21 June, www.bbc.com/news/business-40351859 (archived at https://perma.cc/6X8J-S9P7)

BCG (Boston Consulting Group) (2017) At LEGO, growth and culture are not kid stuff: An Interview with Jørgen Vig Knudstorp, 9 February, www.bcg.com/publications/2017/people-organization-jorgen-vig-knudstorp-lego-growth-culture-not-kid-stuff (archived at https://perma.cc/GHF8-AKBG)

Ben & Jerry's (2021) Flavor graveyard, www.benjerry.com/flavors/flavor-graveyard (archived at https://perma.cc/9GEZ-8YFP)

Benston, G (2003) The quality of corporate financial statements and their auditors before and after Enron, www.cato.org/policy-analysis/quality-corporate-financial-statements-their-auditors-after-enron (archived at https://perma.cc/NCA6-M86U)

Berger, A (2000) The meanings of culture: Culture: Its many meanings, *M/C Journal*, 3 (2)

Berger, E (2021) *Liftoff: Elon Musk and the desperate early days that launched SpaceX*, HarperCollins, London

Bersin, J (2021) Understanding the exciting, new, disrupted labor market, 11 April, https://joshbersin.com/2021/04/understanding-the-new-disrupted-exciting-labor-market/ (archived at https://perma.cc/EJA9-VR3S)

Bjerke, L and Johansson, S (2015) Patterns of innovation and collaboration in small and large firms, *The Annals of Regional Science*

Black, L (1994) Viacom ups studio bid with merger, *Independent*, 8 January, www.independent.co.uk/news/business/viacom-ups-studio-bid-with-merger-1405426.html (archived at https://perma.cc/A6AU-ACXE)

Bloomberg Markets (2019) China's insurance giant is morphing into a tech company, 2 December, www.bloomberg.com/news/articles/2019-12-02/ping-an-co-ceos-talk-about-the-chinese-insurer-s-move-into-tech (archived at https://perma.cc/DRN5-M5CH)

Bolles, G (2021) *The Next Rules of Work*, Kogan Page, London

British Airways (2021) Celebrating Concorde, www.britishairways.com/en-es/information/about-ba/history-and-heritage/celebrating-concorde (archived at https://perma.cc/LMX6-CYYY)

Brown, N and Agrawal, T (2013) Kodak emerges from bankruptcy with focus on commercial printing, Reuters, 3 September, www.reuters.com/article/us-eastmankodak-emergence-idUSBRE98213220130903 (archived at https://perma.cc/929B-7RW7)

Brown, S, Jones, G and Ashcroft, P (2020) *The Curious Advantage*, Laïki Publishing

Burgueño Salas, E (2021) Market share of the lead ride-hailing companies in the United States from September 2017 to July 2021, Statista Research Department, 20 October, www.statista.com/statistics/910704/market-share-of-rideshare-companies-united-states/ (archived at https://perma.cc/ESX7-52HS)

Cambridge Dictionary (2021) Concorde fallacy, https://dictionary.cambridge.org/
dictionary/english/concorde-fallacy (archived at https://perma.cc/X58V-CD64)

CarePay (2021) About us, www.carepay.com/about (archived at https://perma.
cc/3PPE-TQJ2)

Ceci, L (2021) Number of apps available in leading app stores 2021, Statista
Research Department, 10 September

Chang, K and Roston, M (2021) SpaceX successfully lands prototype of Mars and
Moon rocket after test flight, *The New York Times*, 5 May, www.nytimes.
com/2021/05/05/science/spacex-starship-launch.html (archived at https://perma.
cc/3FUV-EHDL)

Chapman, J (2000) Internet may be just a passing fad as millions give up on it,
Daily Mail, 5 December

Christie's (2021) Beeple: The first 5000 days, 11 March, https://onlineonly.christies.
com/s/beeple-first-5000-days/lots/2020 (archived at https://perma.cc/S6XW-
3ZRD)

Clark, D (2021) Average company lifespan on Standard and Poor's 500 Index from
1965 to 2030, Statista Research Department, www.statista.com/statistics/1259275/
average-company-lifespan/ (archived at https://perma.cc/2Z8L-QLZM)

Clark, T (2020) *The 4 Stages of Psychological Safety: Defining the path to
inclusion and innovation*, Berrett-Koehler, Oakland

Connell-Waite, J (2014) Nike's management philosophy revealed, LinkedIn, 4
November, www.linkedin.com/pulse/20141103230923-9245190-nike-s-
management-philosophy-revealed/ (archived at https://perma.cc/32PY-TVLU)

Corporate Leadership Council (now Gartner) (2002) *Building the High-
Performance Workforce: A quantitative analysis of the effectiveness of
performance management strategies*, https://marble-arch-online-courses.s3.
amazonaws.com/CLC_Building_the_High_Performance_Workforce_A_
Quantitative_Analysis_of_the_Effectiveness_of_Performance_Management_
Strategies1.pdf (archived at https://perma.cc/L8G8-36UV)

Coyle, D (2019) *The Culture Code: The secrets of highly successful groups*,
Random House, New York City

Credit Suisse (2017) Corporate longevity: Index turnover and corporate
performance, 7 February, https://plus.credit-suisse.com/rpc4/
ravDocView?docid=V6y0SB2AF-WEr1ce (archived at https://perma.cc/63Q9-
GVVJ)

Croswell, L (2021) How engagement and innovation work together, Culture Amp,
https://cultureamp.com/blog/engagement-and-innovation (archived at https://
perma.cc/4QWB-LGHU)

Daisley, B (2019) *The Joy of Work*, Random House Business, New York City

Davis, D (2021) Premier League chiefs 'ready to roll over current TV deal worth £1.5bn a year into next season' with 'uncertainty over return of mass crowds complicating talks with broadcasters over package', *Daily Mail*, 28 April, www.dailymail.co.uk/sport/football/article-9518947/Premier-League-chiefs-ready-roll-current-TV-deal-season.html (archived at https://perma.cc/H2VM-ASD6)

Davis, J (2017) How LEGO clicked: The super brand that reinvented itself, *Guardian*, 4 June, www.theguardian.com/lifeandstyle/2017/jun/04/how-lego-clicked-the-super-brand-that-reinvented-itself (archived at https://perma.cc/6L83-KSKR)

De Jong, M, Marston, N and Roth, E (2015) The eight essentials of innovation, McKinsey & Company, 1 April, www.mckinsey.com/business-functions/strategy-and-corporate-finance/our-insights/the-eight-essentials-of-innovation (archived at https://perma.cc/W9TQ-TVXX)

Deloitte Touche Tohmatsu (2014) *Delivering Superior Customer Experience in China: The essential ingredient to building customer loyalty*, www2.deloitte.com/content/dam/Deloitte/tr/Documents/consumer-business/delivering-superior-customer-experience-in-china-customer-loyalty.pdf (archived at https://perma.cc/EA7A-XRY5)

Deloitte Touche Tohmatsu (2019) Technology and the boardroom: A CIO's guide to engaging the board, 22 February, www2.deloitte.com/us/en/insights/focus/cio-insider-business-insights/boards-technology-fluency-cio-guide.html (archived at https://perma.cc/AWH9-7AJU)

Diamandis, P (2018) Connecting 8 billion by 2024, 22 July, www.diamandis.com/blog/connecting-8-billion (archived at https://perma.cc/W9FZ-NUZS)

Dickey, M (2018) Uber hits 10 billion trips, TechCrunch, 24 July, https://techcrunch.com/2018/07/24/uber-hits-10-billion-trips/ (archived at https://perma.cc/3XRH-4YUQ)

Disney Fandom (2021) Bob Iger's thoughts of WDAS in 2006, 6 January, https://disney.fandom.com/f/p/4400000000000296776 (archived at https://perma.cc/5RJL-VQB3)

Dugan, R and Gabriel, K (2013) 'Special forces' innovation: How DARPA attacks problems, *Harvard Business Review*, October, https://hbr.org/2013/10/special-forces-innovation-how-darpa-attacks-problems (archived at https://perma.cc/3RTH-QDUL)

Durso, J (1968) Fearless Fosbury flops to glory, *The New York Times*, 20 October, http://archive.nytimes.com/www.nytimes.com/packages/html/sports/year_in_sports/10.20.html (archived at https://perma.cc/WV4W-8ARQ)

Dweck, C (2007) *Mindset: The new psychology of success*, Ballantine Books, New York City

Edmondson, A (1999) Psychological safety and learning behavior in work teams, *Administrative Science Quarterly*, 44 (2), pp 350–83

EFMA (2021) Insurance innovation: Fostering a revolution with Ping An, 26 October, www.efma.com/index.php/article/16647-fostering-a-revolution-ping-an (archived at https://perma.cc/5FJK-CQAM)

Elfond, G (2021) How innovative incentive and recognition programs motivate employees to do more, Forbes, 13 August, www.forbes.com/sites/forbestechcouncil/2021/08/13/how-innovative-incentive-and-recognition-programs-motivate-employees-to-do-more/ (archived at https://perma.cc/Y2S6-PPL7)

EMSI (2021) Jobs posting dashboard, www.economicmodeling.com/job-posting-dashboard/ (archived at https://perma.cc/B7RR-RNDA)

Financial Times (2006) Full text of Warren Buffett's memorandum – 27th September 2006, 9 October, www.ft.com/content/48312832-57d4-11db-be9f-0000779e2340 (archived at https://perma.cc/9HUC-J8GZ)

Finding Nemo (2003) Directed by Andrew Stanton [Film], Buena Vista Pictures Distribution

Fisher, C, Amabile, T and Pillemer, J (2021) How to help (without micromanaging), *Harvard Business Review*, January–February, https://hbr.org/2021/01/how-to-help-without-micromanaging (archived at https://perma.cc/QBB8-FTHY)

Fisk, P (2021) Zhong An: China's first online insurance brand, with a quirky approach to selling, www.peterfisk.com/gamechanger/zhong-an/ (archived at https://perma.cc/X9PT-6B25)

Fond (2020) Best mission statements, 13 February, www.fond.co/blog/best-mission-statements/ (archived at https://perma.cc/HL5Q-J5NZ)

Frost and Sullivan (2019) Global ranking of airlines according to digital readiness, www.frost.com/frost-perspectives/global-ranking-of-airlines-according-to-digital-readiness/ (archived at https://perma.cc/6T7B-HD8J)

Frozen (2013) Directed by Chris Buck and Jennifer Lee [Film], Walt Disney Studios Motion Pictures

Fry, R (2018) Millennials are the largest generation in the US labor force, Pew Research Center, 11 April, www.pewresearch.org/fact-tank/2018/04/11/millennials-largest-generation-us-labor-force/ (archived at https://perma.cc/BD38-EBRJ)

Fry, R (2020) The pace of Boomer retirements has accelerated in the past year, Pew Research Center, 9 November, www.pewresearch.org/fact-tank/2020/11/09/the-pace-of-boomer-retirements-has-accelerated-in-the-past-year/ (archived at https://perma.cc/5A6B-8AC5)

Gartner (2019) 3 culture conversations every CEO must have with the head of HR, www.gartner.com/en/human-resources/trends/3-culture-conversations-ceo-must-have-chro (archived at https://perma.cc/G6GW-2XUD)

Gentry, W, Weber, T and Sadri, G (2007) *Empathy in the Workplace: A tool for effective leadership*, https://cclinnovation.org/wp-content/uploads/2020/03/empathyintheworkplace.pdf (archived at https://perma.cc/94AL-ARZF)

Gino, F (2018) *Rebel Talent: Why it pays to break the rules at work and in life*, Dey Street Books, New York City

Glassdoor (2021) 40+ stats for companies to keep in mind for 2021, www.glassdoor.com/employers/resources/hr-and-recruiting-stats/ (archived at https://perma.cc/2FDY-T6UQ)

Greeven, M, Duke, L, Yang, J and Wei, W (2019) *The Role of Ping An Technology in Enabling Ping An Group's Digital Ecosystem*, Harvard Business Publishing Education, Boston, Massachusetts

Guardian staff and agencies (2021) 'Just magical': Joy for Tamberi and Barshim as they opt to share gold in men's high jump, *Guardian*, 2 August, www.theguardian.com/sport/2021/aug/02/tamberi-barshim-share-olympic-gold-mens-high-jump-reaction (archived at https://perma.cc/53Z5-P6A5)

Hamel, G and Zanini, M (2020) *Humanocracy: Creating organizations as amazing as the people inside them*, Harvard Business Review Press, Brighton

Hangar 51 (2020) Homepage, www.hangar51.com (archived at https://perma.cc/9GFP-AR2E)

Harvard Business Review (2012) Sally Ride, https://hbr.org/2012/09/sally-ride (archived at https://perma.cc/J8ZL-AHH9)

Harvard Business Review (2017) *Empathy* (HBR Emotional Intelligence Series), Harvard Business Review Press, Boston, Massachusetts

Harwood, W (2021) SpaceX Falcon 9 boosts record 143 satellites into orbit on 'rideshare' mission, CBS News, 25 January, www.cbsnews.com/news/spacex-143-satellites-falcon-9-rocket-rideshare/ (archived at https://perma.cc/X7WK-755G)

Hastings, R and Meyer, E (2020) *No Rules Rules: Netflix and the culture of reinvention*, Penguin Press, London

Heen, S and Stone, D (2014) *Thanks for the Feedback: The science and art of receiving feedback well (even when it is off-base, unfair, poorly delivered, and frankly you're not in the mood*, Viking, New York City

Herway, J (2017) How to create a culture of psychological safety, Gallup, 7 December, www.gallup.com/workplace/236198/create-culture-psychological-safety.aspx (archived at https://perma.cc/LV9Z-V7HV)

Hsieh, T (2010) How Zappos infuses culture using core values, *Harvard Business Review*, 24 May, https://hbr.org/2010/05/how-zappos-infuses-culture-using-core-values (archived at https://perma.cc/4TDU-DU85)

Humphrey, D (1994) Delivering deposit services: ATMs versus branches, *Economic Quarterly*, 59–81

Hunter, A (2020) Trust, patience and hard work: How Jürgen Klopp transformed Liverpool, *Guardian*, 26 June, www.theguardian.com/football/2020/jun/26/trust-patience-and-hard-work-how-jurgen-klopp-transformed-liverpool (archived at https://perma.cc/9VLK-X6Q8)

IBM (2021) Deep Blue, www.ibm.com/ibm/history/ibm100/us/en/icons/deepblue/ (archived at https://perma.cc/3YFV-6C7W)

IMDB (Internet Movie Database) (1995) *Toy Story*, www.imdb.com/title/ tt0114709/ (archived at https://perma.cc/42EC-XCZG)

Isaac, M (2017) How Uber deceives the authorities worldwide, *The New York Times*, 3 March, www.nytimes.com/2017/03/03/technology/uber-greyball-program-evade-authorities.html (archived at https://perma.cc/TG8G-RQAW)

Isaac, M (2019) *Super Pumped: The battle for Uber*, W. W. Norton and Company, New York City

Jacobides, M and Reeves, M (2020) Adapt your business to the new reality: Start by understanding how habits have changed, *Harvard Business Review*, September–October, https://hbr.org/2020/09/adapt-your-business-to-the-new-reality (archived at https://perma.cc/8Z48-Q53T)

JLABS (2021) About us, https://jlabs.jnjinnovation.com/vision (archived at https://perma.cc/LBU9-NPKY)

Johnson, G, Scholes, K, Whittington, R, Angwin, D and Regner, P (2017) *Exploring Corporate Strategy*, Pearson, London

Johnson, J (2021) Global digital population as of January 2021, Statista Research Department, 10 September, www.statista.com/statistics/617136/digital-population-worldwide/ (archived at https://perma.cc/29VT-3L2P)

Karlinsky, N and Stead, J (2018) How a door became a desk, and a symbol of Amazon, Amazon, 17 January, www.aboutamazon.com/news/workplace/how-a-door-became-a-desk-and-a-symbol-of-amazon (archived at https://perma.cc/4J59-8JAA)

Kaufman, S (2011) Why inspiration matters, *Harvard Business Review*, 8 November, https://hbr.org/2011/11/why-inspiration-matters (archived at https://perma.cc/894E-9BPL)

Kokalitcheva, K (2015) Uber completes 1 billion rides, Fortune, 31 December, https://fortune.com/2015/12/30/uber-completes-1-billion-rides/ (archived at https://perma.cc/6U2R-2RM3)

Koss, H (2020) 7 leadership lessons from Netflix CEO Reed Hastings' new book, Built In, 15 September, https://builtin.com/company-culture/netflix-book (archived at https://perma.cc/RP4V-EFUM)

Krishna, A (2020) I pledge to support my fellow IBMers working from home during Covid-19, LinkedIn, 2 May, www.linkedin.com/pulse/i-pledge-support-my-fellow-ibmers-working-from-home-during-krishna/ (archived at https://perma.cc/W3RQ-3EH9)

Kroeber, A, Kluckhohn, C and Untereiner, W (1952) *Culture: A critical review of concepts and definitions*, Peabody Museum, Cambridge

La Monica, P (2006) Disney buys Pixar: House of Mouse is teaming up with Pixar in a $7.4 billion deal. Steve Jobs to become board member at Disney, 25 January, https://money.cnn.com/2006/01/24/news/companies/disney_pixar_deal/ (archived at https://perma.cc/M6ZS-R4H3)

Latham, G Locke, E (1991) A theory of goal setting and task performance, *The Academy of Management Review*, 16 (2)

Lee, D (2013) Nokia: The rise and fall of a mobile giant, BBC News, 3 September, www.bbc.co.uk/news/technology-23947212 (archived at https://perma.cc/884R-LKRH)

Leicester City Football Club (2020) LCFC training ground in numbers, 26 December, www.lcfc.com/news/1950709/leicester-citys-spectacular-new-training-ground-the-numbers (archived at https://perma.cc/K5UU-YM37)

Lewis, N (2019) Walmart revolutionizes its training with virtual reality, SHRM, 22 July, www.shrm.org/resourcesandtools/hr-topics/technology/pages/virtual-reality-revolutionizes-walmart-training.aspx (archived at https://perma.cc/E6G4-UV5D)

LG (2021) LG hosts tech leaders in virtual CES 'Future Talk' on the value of open innovation in a new era, 13 January, www.lg.com/us/press-release/lg-hosts-tech-leaders-in-virtual-ces-future-talk-on-the-value-of-open-innovation-in-a-new-era (archived at https://perma.cc/HH48-JZB7)

LG Corporation (2021) LG's newest in-vehicle infotainment system to debut in Renault Mégane E-Tech Electric, 1 November, www.lg.com/global/mobility/press-release/lgs-newest-in-vehicle-infotainment-system-to-debut-in-renault-megane-e-tech-electric (archived at https://perma.cc/8LE4-KTWD)

Luca (2021) Directed by Enrico Casarosa [Film], Walt Disney Studios Motion Pictures

Mangel, M and Samaniego, F (1984) Abraham Wald's work on aircraft survivability, *Journal of the American Statistical Association*, 79 (386), pp 259–67

Manheimer, E (2013) *Twelve Patients: Life and death at Bellevue Hospital*, Grand Central Publishing, New York City

Manu Cornet (2011) Organizational charts, Bonkers World, 27 June, https://bonkersworld.net/organizational-charts (archived at https://perma.cc/2GLG-LQNV)

Mari Tottoc, J (2021) 2 years worth of digital transformation in 2 months for Microsoft, Yahoo Finance, 8 February, https://finance.yahoo.com/news/2-years-worth-digital-transformation-170251059.html (archived at https://perma.cc/NCW3-FVNF)

Marriott (2021) J Willard Marriott, www.marriott.com/culture-and-values/j-willard-marriott.mi (archived at https://perma.cc/FW89-JPYN)

Mastercard (2019) *Annual Report*, https://s25.q4cdn.com/479285134/files/doc_financials/2019/ar/2019-Annual-Report-on-Form-10-K.pdf (archived at https://perma.cc/GKM6-YEQE)

Masterclass (2019) Bob Iger teaches business strategy and leadership, 14 November, www.masterclass.com/classes/bob-iger-teaches-business-strategy-and-leadership (archived at https://perma.cc/2K4C-PTLJ)

Mayor of London (2021) Taxis in London, 17 March, www.london.gov.uk/ questions/2021/1202 (archived at https://perma.cc/42ML-Q7RG)

McCarthy, M (2021) Gympass, the corporate wellness unicorn, raises a $220m series E, 29 June, https://techcrunch.com/2021/06/29/gympass-the-corporate-wellness-unicorn-raises-a-220m-series-e/ (archived at https://perma.cc/ PXU9-KDY7)

McCord, P (2018) *Powerful: Building a culture of freedom and responsibility*, Silicon Guild, San Francisco

McKinsey & Company (2018) Building a tech-enabled ecosystem: An interview with Ping An's Jessica Tan, *McKinsey Quarterly*, December www.mckinsey. com/~/media/McKinsey/Featured%20Insights/China/Building%20a%20 tech%20enabled%20ecosystem%20An%20interview%20with%20Ping%20 Ans%20Jessica%20Tan/Building-a-tech-enabled-ecosystem-An-interview-with-Ping-Ans-Jessica-Tan.pdf (archived at https://perma.cc/6T9L-YUNT)

McKinsey & Company (2021) Psychological safety and the critical role of leadership development, McKinsey, 11 February, www.mckinsey.com/business-functions/people-and-organizational-performance/our-insights/ psychological-safety-and-the-critical-role-of-leadership-development (archived at https://perma.cc/53M4-97J3)

McKinsey Digital (2021) The top trends in tech, www.mckinsey.com/business-functions/mckinsey-digital/our-insights/the-top-trends-in-tech (archived at https://perma.cc/8WMJ-KSEK)

Minor, D, Brook, P and Bernoff, J (2017) Are innovative companies more profitable? MIT Sloan Management Review, 28 December, https://sloanreview. mit.edu/article/are-innovative-companies-more-profitable/ (archived at https:// perma.cc/E963-MJ62)

Moneyball (2011) Directed by Bennett Miller [Film], Sony Pictures Releasing

Munarriz, R (2008) Blockbuster CEO has answers: An interview with Jim Keyes shows his confidence, The Motley Fool, 10 December, www.fool.com/investing/ general/2008/12/10/blockbuster-ceo-has-answers.aspx (archived at https:// perma.cc/4E73-4YL3)

Nadella, S (2017) *Hit Refresh: Our quest to rediscover Microsoft's soul and imagine a better future for everyone*, HarperCollins, New York City

Nasdaq (2021) Ping Identity wins Glassdoor Employees' Choice Award, 13 January, www.nasdaq.com/press-release/ping-identity-wins-glassdoor-employees-choice-award-2021-01-13 (archived at https://perma.cc/2JYD-XU5E)

Netflix (2009) Culture, www.slideshare.net/reed2001/culture-1798664 (archived at https://perma.cc/EG4W-DGEU)

Netflix (2021a) Q1-21 shareholder letter, https://s22.q4cdn.com/959853165/files/ doc_financials/2021/q1/FINAL-Q1-21-Shareholder-Letter.pdf (archived at https://perma.cc/B3T4-EH8J)

Netflix (2021b) Netflix culture, https://jobs.netflix.com/culture (archived at https://perma.cc/R552-HHR3)

New Amsterdam (2018–) Executive Producers Peter Horton, David Schulner and Various [TV series], NBC Universal Television Distribution

Nokia (2007) *Nokia in 2007: Review by the Board of Directors and Nokia Annual Accounts 2007*, www.nokia.com/system/files/files/request-nokia-in-2007-pdf.pdf (archived at https://perma.cc/CPT5-5BLH)

Novartis (2021) People and culture, www.novartis.com/about/strategy/people-and-culture (archived at https://perma.cc/B7Z4-N7BW)

O'Connell, A (2009) Crisis management: LEGO CEO Jørgen Vig Knudstorp on leading through survival and growth, *Harvard Business Review*, January, https://hbr.org/2009/01/lego-ceo-jorgen-vig-knudstorp-on-leading-through-survival-and-growth (archived at https://perma.cc/RBZ6-DDST)

Olano, G (2020) Ping An identifies four key growth areas, Insurance Business Asia, 15 September, www.insurancebusinessmag.com/asia/news/breaking-news/ping-an-identifies-four-key-growth-areas-233495.aspx (archived at https://perma.cc/TPU8-R7CZ)

Olympics (2021) Ellery Clark, https://olympics.com/en/athletes/ellery-clark (archived at https://perma.cc/PH3Q-USBJ)

O'Neill, A (2021a) Gold medal winning heights in the men's and women's high jump at the summer Olympics from 1896 to 2020, Statista Research Department, 10 August, www.statista.com/statistics/1100364/olympics-high-jump-gold-medal-heights-since-1896/ (archived at https://perma.cc/Y2SA-MEYQ)

O'Neill, A (2021b) Life expectancy at birth worldwide 2019, Statista Research Department, www.statista.com/statistics/805060/life-expectancy-at-birth-worldwide/ (archived at https://perma.cc/4HXL-3M8T)

Pearson, K (2016) *The Life, Letters and Labors of Francis Galton*, Volume 2, Palala Press, United States

Pélissié du Rausas, M, Manyika, J, Hazan, E, Bughin, J, Chui, M and Said, R (2011) Internet matters: The net's sweeping impact on growth, jobs, and prosperity, McKinsey & Company, 1 May, www.mckinsey.com/industries/technology-media-and-telecommunications/our-insights/internet-matters# (archived at https://perma.cc/GDU9-8K4G)

Pell, G (2018) The perennial mindset in the era of ageless with Gina Pell, Berkley Arts and Design, 7 May, www.youtube.com/watch?v=Gio5QirB7Lc (archived at https://perma.cc/MA3B-EASL)

Ping An (2021) About us, https://group.pingan.com/about_us.html (archived at https://perma.cc/HW32-DCJS)

Pirie, M (2019) When Concorde first took flight, Adam Smith Institute, 2 March, www.adamsmith.org/blog/when-concorde-first-took-flight-1 (archived at https://perma.cc/32BM-TK5C)

PR Newswire (2013) DARPA awards Moderna Therapeutics a grant for up to $25 million to develop Messenger RNA Therapeutics, 2 October, https://www. prnewswire.com/news-releases/darpa-awards-moderna-therapeutics-a-grant-for-up-to-25-million-to-develop-messenger-rna-therapeutics-226115821.html (archived at https://perma.cc/7BVG-LXTW)

PR Newswire (2021) 'Easier, faster and more affordable': Ping An Good Doctor's new strategy builds on solid foundation, 24 October, www.prnewswire.com/ news-releases/easier-faster-and-more-affordable-ping-an-good-doctors-new-strategy-builds-on-solid-foundation-301407238.html (archived at https://perma. cc/Q7D6-C2YG)

Raymundo, O (2014) Richard Branson: Companies should put employees first: The Virgin founder shares how making employees the top priority can bring benefits for both customers and investors, Inc., 28 October, www.inc.com/oscar-raymundo/richard-branson-companies-should-put-employees-first.html (archived at https://perma.cc/86T9-58EB)

Reuters (2018) Ping An's Good Doctor unit raises $1.1 billion in Hong Kong IPO: Sources, 27 April, www.reuters.com/article/us-pingan-hlthcr-tc-ipo-idUSKBN1HY04S (archived at https://perma.cc/AJA2-KUMA)

Ruddick, G (2015) VW admits emissions scandal was caused by 'whole chain' of failures, *Guardian*, 10 December, www.theguardian.com/business/2015/dec/10/ volkswagen-emissions-scandal-systematic-failures-hans-dieter-potsch (archived at https://perma.cc/39LK-7KKC)

Scott, J (2011) Nokia R&D spend outweighs Apple and HTC, IT Pro, 4 February, www.itpro.co.uk/630721/nokia-rd-spend-outweighs-apple-and-htc (archived at https://perma.cc/978Z-GTRP)

Sheetz, M (2021) SpaceX's Starship prototype again explodes on landing attempt after successful launch, CNBC, 2 February, www.cnbc.com/2021/02/02/ spacex-starship-sn9-explodes-on-attempted-landing.html (archived at https:// perma.cc/B45T-8V9J)

Shellenbarger, S (2019) The dangers of hiring for cultural fit: Employers often aim to hire people they think will be a good fit, but their efforts can easily veer into a ditch where new hires all look, think and act alike, *The Wall Street Journal*, 23 September, www.wsj.com/articles/the-dangers-of-hiring-for-cultural-fit-11569231000 (archived at https://perma.cc/7HSE-LJLQ)

Shontell, A (2013) Sheryl Sandberg: 'The most important document ever to come out of the Valley', 4 February, www.businessinsider.in/SHERYL-SANDBERG-The-Most-Important-Document-Ever-To-Come-Out-Of-The-Valley/ articleshow/21390606.cms (archived at https://perma.cc/EQ2J-ZYEF)

Sinek, S (2009) How great leaders inspire action, TED, September, www.ted.com/ talks/simon_sinek_how_great_leaders_inspire_action?language=en (archived at https://perma.cc/K3SC-F52X)

Slotta, D (2021a) Number of employees at Ping An Insurance from 2010 to 2020, Statista Research Department, 14 July, www.statista.com/statistics/284350/china-number-of-employees-at-ping-an-insurance/ (archived at https://perma.cc/BQ3L-JXKK)

Slotta, D (2021b) Number of smartphone users in China from 2015 to 2020 with a forecast until 2026, 16 August, www.statista.com/statistics/467160/forecast-of-smartphone-users-in-china/ (archived at https://perma.cc/9MVB-6VB2)

Smith, D and Alexander R (1988) *Fumbling the Future: How Xerox invented then ignored the first personal computer*, William Morrow and Company, New York City

Sorenson, A (2020) Covid-19: A message to Marriott International associates from President and CEO Arne Sorenson, YouTube, 20 March, www.youtube.com/watch?v=SprFgoU6aO0 (archived at https://perma.cc/K9KL-NT8R)

Soul (2020) Directed by Pete Docter [Film], Walt Disney Studios Motion Pictures

Statista Research Department (2013) Global market share held by Nokia smartphones from 1st quarter 2007 to 2nd quarter 2013, www.statista.com/statistics/263438/market-share-held-by-nokia-smartphones-since-2007/ (archived at https://perma.cc/LXQ7-48U5)

Stockport County (2021) Club part company with Jim Gannon, 21 January, www.stockportcounty.com/club-part-company-with-jim-gannon/ (archived at https://perma.cc/6HAT-GM3V)

Surowiecki, J (2004) *The Wisdom of Crowds: Why the many are smarter than the few and how collective wisdom shapes business, economies, societies and nations*, Doubleday, New York City

Talgam, I (2009) Lead like the great conductors, TED, July, www.ted.com/talks/itay_talgam_lead_like_the_great_conductors?language=en (archived at https://perma.cc/T85Z-JPK3)

The Economist (2020) How Ping An, an insurer, became a fintech super-app, 3 December, www.economist.com/finance-and-economics/2020/12/03/how-ping-an-an-insurer-became-a-fintech-super-app (archived at https://perma.cc/Q87T-MS8B)

The Economist (2021) A growing number of governments hope to clone America's DARPA: They will not succeed unless they adopt the spirit which motivates it, 5 June, www.economist.com/science-and-technology/2021/06/03/a-growing-number-of-governments-hope-to-clone-americas-darpa (archived at https://perma.cc/J4AA-B5T3)

The Good Place (2016–20) Executive Produced by Michael Schur, David Miner, Morgan Sackett and Drew Goddard [TV series], NBC Universal Television Distribution

The LEGO Group (2004) *Annual Report 2004: LEGO Group*, www.lego.com/cdn/cs/aboutus/assets/blt07abb4b8a3da3f39/Annual_Report_2004_ENG.pdf (archived at https://perma.cc/U7PC-LYXZ)

The Pixar Story (2007) Directed by Leslie Iwerks [Documentary], Walt Disney Studios Motion Pictures

The Sunday Times (2021) JK Rowling net worth: Sunday Times Rich List 2021, 21 May, www.thetimes.co.uk/article/sunday-times-rich-list-jk-rowling-net-worth-rhrbq7ctc (archived at https://perma.cc/W5KY-JVXX)

The World Bank (2019) Fertility rate, total (births per woman), https://data.worldbank.org/indicator/SP.DYN.TFRT.IN (archived at https://perma.cc/4878-T2MN)

The World Bank (2020a) Automated teller machines (ATMs) (per 100,000 adults), https://data.worldbank.org/indicator/FB.ATM.TOTL.P5 (archived at https://perma.cc/Q4NB-MT4R)

The World Bank (2020b) Commercial bank branches (per 100,000 adults), https://data.worldbank.org/indicator/FB.CBK.BRCH.P5 (archived at https://perma.cc/CFZ2-CEME)

TopResume (2020) New findings by TopResume reveal what really matters most to job seekers, 31 August, www.topresume.com/career-advice/press-2020-08-31 (archived at https://perma.cc/3KGL-ZYR7)

Toy Story (1995) Directed by John Lasseter [Film], Buena Vista Pictures Distribution

Tsai, S, Wendt, J, Donnelly, R, de Jong, G and Ahmed, F (2005) Age at retirement and long term survival of an industrial population: Prospective cohort study, *British Medical Journal*, 29 October, 331 (7523), p 995

Uber (2021) The history of Uber: Uber's timeline, www.uber.com/newsroom/history/ (archived at https://perma.cc/9GNT-ABFD)

United States House Committee on Transportation and Infrastructure (2020) *Final Committee Report: The design, development and certification of the Boeing 737 MAX*, September, https://transportation.house.gov/imo/media/doc/2020.09.15%20FINAL%20737%20MAX%20Report%20for%20Public%20Release.pdf (archived at https://perma.cc/6DG9-4B23)

Vaynerchuk, G (2017a) The cream rises to the top in coffee and in personal branding, www.garyvaynerchuk.com/cream-rises-top-coffee-personal-branding-veecap/ (archived at https://perma.cc/A9ZM-GTMW)

Vaynerchuk, G (2017b) Wine tasting in brown paper bags, www.garyvaynerchuk.com/brownpaperbags/ (archived at https://perma.cc/X8H6-38EF)

Vaynerchuk, G (2020) Gary Vaynerchuk: Now, more than ever, is the time for businesses to think about innovation, 31 March, www.cnbc.com/2020/03/31/gary-vaynerchuk-now-is-the-time-for-businesses-to-think-about-innovation.html (archived at https://perma.cc/6CMZ-EFYX)

Vaynerchuk, G (2021) *Twelve and a Half*, Harper Business, New York City

VeeFriends (2021) Frequently asked questions, https://veefriends.com/ (archived at https://perma.cc/9BBZ-9JML)

Virkus, S (2009) The concept of leadership, www.tlu.ee/~sirvir/Leadership/The%20 Concept%20of%20Leadership/definitions_of_leadership.html (archived at https://perma.cc/T8MC-NXFM)

Walmart (2021) About, https://corporate.walmart.com/about (archived at https://perma.cc/66KN-5HVV)

Wang, E (2020) Ping An's Global Voyager Fund mulls roping in third-party LPs in new fund, Deal Street Asia, 1 October, www.dealstreetasia.com/stories/ping-an-global-voyager-fund-2-208390/ (archived at https://perma.cc/DEV3-GMRJ)

WD-40 Company (2021) Fascinating facts you never learned in school, www.wd40.com/history/ (archived at https://perma.cc/J6KE-R3B3)

Wikipedia (2021) Wikipedia: Size of Wikipedia, https://en.wikipedia.org/wiki/Wikipedia:Size_of_Wikipedia (archived at https://perma.cc/SLD4-LYJY)

World Economic Forum (2015) *Collaborative Innovation: Transforming business, driving growth*, www3.weforum.org/docs/WEF_Collaborative_Innovation_report_2015.pdf (archived at https://perma.cc/97JL-48S2)

World Population Review (2021) China population 2021 live, https://worldpopulationreview.com/countries/china-population (archived at https://perma.cc/L2CL-G2NC)

World Wide Web Foundation (2021) History of the web, https://webfoundation.org/about/vision/history-of-the-web/ (archived at https://perma.cc/P3FL-MBKA)

XPRIZE (2020) XPRIZE announces winners of million dollar next-gen mask challenge to reveal the next generation of face masks, 22 December, www.xprize.org/articles/xprize-next-gen-mask-winners (archived at https://perma.cc/5HVB-T72Q)

XPRIZE (2021) $100m prize for carbon removal, www.xprize.org/prizes/elonmusk (archived at https://perma.cc/QM8D-9EEP)

Y Combinator (2017) Hiring and culture with Patrick and John Collison and Ben Silbermann, Stanford University, YouTube, www.youtube.com/watch?v=kTS7OIAMunM (archived at https://perma.cc/AQ4T-L6VV)

Yahoo Finance (2021a) Microsoft Corporation (MSFT) NasdaqGS share price, 13 November, https://finance.yahoo.com/quote/MSFT?p=MSFT (archived at https://perma.cc/57X7-V2Q3)

Yahoo Finance (2021b) Uber Technologies Inc. (UBER) NYSE USD market capitalization, 13 November, https://finance.yahoo.com/quote/UBER/ (archived at https://perma.cc/7G7A-AESX)

Yahoo Finance (2021c) WD-40 Company (WDFC), 19 November, https://finance.yahoo.com/quote/wdfc?ltr=1 (archived at https://perma.cc/XH5V-98WK)

Ycharts (2021) Ping An Insurance (Group) Co. of China market cap:138.02B for Nov. 12, 2021 [live updates page], https://ycharts.com/companies/PNGAY/market_cap (archived at https://perma.cc/LJM2-ER4T) [live page]

Yu, H and Feng, Y (2020) How Ping An went from a traditional insurer to become a tech giant, IMD, November, www.imd.org/news/updates/how-ping-an-went-from-a-traditional-insurer-to-become-a-tech-giant/ (archived at https://perma.cc/WW4B-ADPP)

INDEX

Boxes *and* questions for reflection are indexed as such; page numbers in italic indicate figures or tables.

Lightning Source UK Ltd.
Milton Keynes UK
UKHW020639010223
416253UK00004B/11